COMING OF AGE IN JIM CROW DC

Coming of Age in Jim Crow DC

Navigating the Politics of Everyday Life

Paula C. Austin

NEW YORK UNIVERSITY PRESS

New York

NEW YORK UNIVERSITY PRESS
New York
www.nyupress.org

© 2019 by New York University
All rights reserved

ISBN: 978-1-4798-9499-4 (hardback)
ISBN: 978-1-4798-0811-3 (paperback)

For Library of Congress Cataloging-in-Publication data, please contact the Library of Congress.

New York University Press books are printed on acid-free paper, and their binding materials are chosen for strength and durability. We strive to use environmentally responsible suppliers and materials to the greatest extent possible in publishing our books.

Manufactured in the United States of America

10 9 8 7 6 5 4 3 2 1

Also available as an ebook

This project is dedicated to Ena A. Austin and Pearl Shelby Sharpe, two everyday women who inspired and encouraged me to tell (historicized) stories. I miss you and hope you are proud of this. And to Nasia, Ari, and Jordan who, early on, created in me an appreciation for the intellectual capacity of young people.

CONTENTS

Introduction

There is a dearth of traditional records for the thoughts and experiences of black poor and working-class folks and this has informed their presence, their absence, and their misrepresentation in the historical record. As historian Cheryl Hicks notes, ordinary people "rarely [leave] personal documents attesting to their lives and [are] often under-represented in organizations and the press."[1] Centering young black people, too, has been difficult. Sources that allow for young people's voices are scarce and contested.[2] This, of course, is even truer in the study of marginalized poor and working-class (urban) African American youth, who are simultaneously seen as at risk and prone to criminality and deviance because of the *ghetto's* influences.

But this historical manifestation, or lack thereof, is not solely a result of the scarcity of sources. Even in the revisionist period of the late twentieth century, scholars generally avoided the daily lives, the consciousness, and the intellectual production of common folks in an effort to render a portrait of racial progress. Black intellectual histories have spotlighted the ideological framings of black elites, many of whom had very conflicted feelings and ideas about black folk.[3] The histories produced in the period following the civil rights movement's legislative victories, in what was the social history turn, focused on assertions of black human agency. This historiographical project to (re)/(pro)claim black humanity, as historian Walter Johnson argues, resulted in a continuum of accommodation and resistance on which black historical actions were positioned and judged to measure agency. While this may have been a necessary approach in the late twentieth century, to "writ[e] Black humanity as self-determination and resistance," it also "delineated an optical field" that ultimately obscured "other things beyond the categories of the 'agency' debates."[4]

Coming of Age in Jim Crow DC offers alternative, complicated narratives of black young people who lived in Washington, DC, during the interwar period. Some were native Washingtonians, some were recent newcomers from parts south and east. Most lived in tight, overcrowded, and generally impoverished conditions. All were coming of age in the segregated US capital. This project listens to black poor and working-class young people as thinkers, theorists, critics, and commentators as they reckoned with, reconciled, and even played with material and rhetorical lines of demarcation set about them both as young people controlled by their parents and other adults and as African Americans in the racially, spatially, economically, and politically restricted city that was also the United States' emblem of equality.

The "racial protocol" for how black lives could be represented in scholarship "reduce[d] African American experiences to racial politics [and] racial struggle"; it paid little attention to private life, "individual subjectivity," and interiority. It created a "two-dimensionality" and a homogeneity of black life. And as both historian Anastasia Curwood and literary scholar Kevin Quashie note, hiding black interiority from public view can lead to the "belief that Black people lack interior lives altogether."[5] *Coming of Age in Jim Crow DC* uses sociological investigations and community and individual interviews that were conducted in the late Progressive and interwar era to highlight the inner and everyday lives, the self-aware and self-reflective analytic frameworks cultivated and articulated by poor and working-class black young people in an urban and social history of Jim Crow Washington, DC.

Social science literature of this era has generally portrayed marginalized black folks as socially and culturally homogeneous in the aggregate—whether represented as in need of rehabilitation or as proletarianized. These studies have rightfully been criticized for reinscribing conventional frameworks of racial and class identities and for reifying social formations steeped in middle-class norms and values. But because of their intrusiveness into communities and people's personal lives, these materials also give us some access to inner life, to the life of the mind.[6]

For example, seventeen-year-old Floretta Johnson's mother, native Washingtonian Clara Winston Johnson, had a long work history as a laundress and childcare worker that started when she was nine years old. When Clara was interviewed for E. Franklin Frazier's *Negro Youth at the Crossways*, she had clearly made many decisions—about her relationships, about delaying her first marriage, about divorcing her abusive and philandering husband, and about childrearing. She defied both contemporary conventions and her mother's advice, insisting that she wasn't someone "who didn't know her own mind."[7] The meaning and force of Clara's words inspire and animate this book.

Here I borrow the concepts of "interiority" and "infra-ordinary" from poets and literary theorists. Interiority refers to "a consciousness of depth and space within; a sensibility"; "human inwardness";[8] self; selfhood; self-knowledge; self-cultivation; a place of "imagination, fantasy, affect, aesthetics, and sensation"; "an amorphous space located somewhere 'inside' the human body, generating conviction, satisfaction, and identity." It assigns autonomous and authorial subjectivity; it emerges from a place of quiet—at once "irreverent, messy, complicated, representations that have human texture and specificity."[9] Like interiority, the infra-ordinary, "everyday practices we don't always notice" are "essential to the possibility of black futurity," and like interiority, they are already there, "if one is looking to understand it."[10] While always linked to the material world and its attendant realities, the interior, as Quashie notes, is not only a bulwark "against dominance of the social world," but it "has its own sovereignty."[11] For so many of the young people, everyday life was filled with, in Tina Campt's words, "practices of refusal. . . . a range of creative responses to sustained everyday encounters with the exigency and duress" of DC's racialized spatial regime.[12]

By foregrounding interiority and the infra-ordinary, the narratives at the center of this book provide a different understanding of black *urban* life in the early twentieth century, a period most scholars identify as both the Great Migration and inclusive of the New Negro Movement and the origins of black "ghetto" formation. We have come to see urbanization as having had a mostly negative impact on rural black folks who flocked to cities, and cities as places where black families experienced the "breakdown" of "traditional" familial bonds, resulting in an increase in urban vice and crime.[13] But what comes through in these narratives are the ways in which black young working-class and poor people were expertly aware of the economic, spatial, social, and political limitations imposed by the District of Columbia's racially segregationist policies and customs, and their critiques of the juxtaposition of those limitations with the emblematic meanings of the nation's capital.

Young people's answers to social science questions make clear the cultivation and mobilization of their own analytic categories and frames, even for the youngest subject. Sometimes these conceptual frames were in tune with and sometimes they diverged from mainstream middle-class mores as promoted by black and white reformers alike. Individuals articulated spatial, racial, class, and gender identities, complex social relations, and a deep consciousness of selfhood with which they negotiated the contradictions of living in the urbanizing and racially segregated US capital. These musings map onto the history of Washington, DC, just as DC planners worked to create a landscape to establish the city on a global stage, and just as the federal government's physical presence invaded historically black and poor spaces.

DC histories have addressed both its racial segregationist past and the origins of its black urban "ghettoes." This includes the early Federal Writers' Project 1937 DC guidebook and its 1942 edition.[14] Since these early publications, scholarship on the history of black DC has centered mostly on black elite communities, focusing on intellectual advancements, cultural and institutional formations, the proliferation of black economic success in the Northwest, and civic/racial pride and participation in the face of structural deterrents, as well as the struggle against many of these obstacles, one of which resulted in the emergence of Howard University as the central site of New Negro intellectual activity and black knowledge production.[15] This scholarship primarily examined the ways in which DC's middle-class black community, its "leading men and women," fortified their social status, redefined themselves in the face of social discrimination, and mobilized around racial uplift among themselves and for the masses.[16] But the "social breach" between black DC's elite and what W. E. B. Du Bois called the "submerged tenth" was wide. Howard's New Negro intellectual Kelly Miller called it, at the time, "more pronounced than in any other city in the country."[17]

Coming of Age in Jim Crow DC is indebted to three publications that take note of DC's poor and working-class African Americans, and address the juxtaposition of DC's "imagined" and "experienced" landscapes.[18] While not specifically a history of black Washington, Howard Gillette Jr.'s *Between Justice and Beauty* examined the long arc of urban policy and planning that often did not reconcile the social welfare needs of marginalized, mostly African American folks and the capital city's project for aesthetic improvement. Gillette highlighted moments in DC's history—Reconstruction, the Progressive Era, the post–World War II era, and even Black Power—when city planning initiatives sought to address both the needs of the city's "neglected neighbors" and make the capital "worthy of a nation."[19] Gillette foregrounded how DC's urban housing, tax, and redevelopment plans—economic, political, and spatial policies that assigned legal meaning to physical spaces—generally failed. The failures reflected not only the relationship between the federal government's dominance of the local capital city but also the ways in which DC's urban policies and programs both mirrored and influenced national urban policy goals. Gillette makes very clear the geopolitical significance of Washington, DC, and the relationship between "racial control" and "spatial control."[20] DC is a national space, a celebrated and for some a sacred space of commemoration. And it was and continues to be a contested space, a space of confrontation and politics.

Two other publications on the history of Washington, DC, specifically center the lives and experiences of black poor and working people. The first, James Borchert's *Alley Life in Washington*, traced the survival and continuity of southern rural "folkways" within DC's black and poor alley communities. Borchert used materials produced by social scientists and reformers to examine family, religious, and work life. He argued that instead of a "breakdown" of values and organization, there was familial and cultural stability in black residential alley communities. While Borchert found that DC's black alleys were part of the transition from "plantation to ghetto," he asserted that migrants adjusted and adapted to the new urban environment, developed community institutions and broad kinship networks that supported their survival in these enclaves, and were not transient; many lived in alley communities for decades and would have stayed longer if urban renewal had not forced them to move.[21]

The second book, Elizabeth Clark-Lewis's *Living In, Living Out: African American Domestics in Washington, D.C., 1910–1940*, narrated the movement and lives of black women domestic workers out of the South and into DC. Through the oral histories of over eighty women, Clark-Lewis outlined their reasons for migration and charted the social and economic life transformations wrought by the conditions of their new city.[22] "Despite constraints of race, gender, and class," stated Clark-Lewis, "these women were never passive, [or] powerless."[23] They took control of their work lives, and some women were even able to change their socioeconomic status through their domestic work. Migrating black women also brought with them a strong family and work ethic, demonstrating the abilities of black migrants to adapt to modern city lifestyles and circumstances.

Both Borchert and Clark-Lewis intervened in much of the scholarship on black urban ghettoization produced in the 1960s and 1970s, scholarship that privileged political and economic interruptions of community building, family life, traditions, and residents' aspirations. They also feature black poor and working Washingtonian's lived experiences.[24] *Coming of Age in Jim Crow DC* both builds on these foundational works and veers from the latter two books, which focus on rehabilitating disorganized black urban enclaves and restoring agency. Literature on poor black urban communities has, in the words of Craig Steven Wilder, stood "as a long story of protest against legal, political, economic and social barriers to African American community building in the twentieth century city." But "the search for agency always confesses constraints."[25]

This book is less concerned with the presumed constraints of inquiry imposed by sociologists, and I do not aim to add to the refutation of the reports that social scientists and others made from their studies. Rather, I interrogate these raw materials to gather the stories of poor and working-class African American young people, to emphasize the specificity of daily existence and ideologies of self-identification and consciousness that do not relegate the experiences of black youth solely to struggles against or accommodations to the "ghetto." This specificity does not define experiences, actions, feelings, and thoughts simply as evidence of the agency or humanity of black poor and working-class young people. *Coming of Age in Jim Crow DC* attempts to challenge the limiting boundaries of intellectual history, examining the critical role of ideas in navigating structural impediments to full identity formation and expression, even for people deemed both too immature and racially inferior to engage fully in intellectual life.[26] Intellectual history has generally been about scale, about the monumentalism of ideas. But, what do we miss when we employ only "traditional notions of significance?" If we linger in the archival materials, reading at a different register, we can see and hear what is already there.[27] The voices within these pages stress the generative capacities of young black poor and working-class people's interior lives and political will.

Scholarship on black women's lives strongly influences the ways in which black young people's narratives appear within these pages, providing valuable theoretical framings and methodologies for exploring inner and everyday life, and the relationship to the production of ideas. Scholars have not simply "deprivileged" white and male as uninspected categories of gender and racial analysis, or examined the ways in which race, gender, and sexuality have been formulated and articulated. They have foregrounded that these identities are both socially constructed and complex, "embrac[ing] a 'kaleidoscopic' angle of vision": the intersectional quality of identity formation and its relationship to the quotidian, and the instability of categories of race and gender.[28]

This framing is important as it reminds us that our identities, our always multiple identities, are not merely those structured around our relationships with the state—how we are either privileged or limited by it, how we are complicit with or are agents in resisting it. Rather, we interact with these structures just as they interact with us: we internalize them, externalize them, ignore them, form and reform sensibilities and notions of ourselves that, while they might always be within these structures, also take these structures for granted, use them as something constructive, and negotiate with them both actually and with their abstractions. In this way, our multiple identities are both performative *and* not solely public.[29] Through our engagement and disengagement with the structures within which we live, we develop our identities, our perspectives, experiences, feelings, beliefs, desires, the analytic categories and conceptualizations by which we live. Specifically, this theoretical understanding does not limit black subjectivity to its social and political relevance, allowing it only to tell us something about race, racism, violence, struggle, or triumph.[30] It allows for the range of capacities of subjectivity.

I also draw my methodological approach from slavery and postcolonial studies, and from labor histories of women.[31] Scholars in these fields interrogate sources not meant to illuminate certain voices, reading archival materials critically and "against [their] limits."[32] In so doing, distinctions between the everyday survival strategies of individuals and collective resistance are collapsed.[33] Instead, changing understandings and definitions of freedom, of "working-class consciousness," of the cultivation of leisure practices, and the ways in which identities were not solely centered on labor and work become foregrounded.[34] This literature builds a social history of governing ideas and political frameworks: an intellectual history that considers the relationship between ideologies and the material, political, and social realities in which they are developed, between the everyday and the production of ideas. Similarly, the emerging interdisciplinary field on black youth and girlhood provides important bolstering to *Coming of Age in Jim Crow DC*.[35]

Black childhood has been a mostly underexamined subfield in the history of young people in the United States. In the mid-1990s, significant scholarship filled this gap, highlighting the lost childhoods of enslaved young people subjected at an early age to "work, terror, injustice, and arbitrary power."[36] Wilma King's collection of chronological essays in *African American Childhoods* brought to the fore voices of and about black children from the colonial period through to the civil rights movement, examining "how major events impacted or changed the lives of Black children."[37] King made an important argument for the variegation of African American childhood experiences, echoing scholar Steven Mintz's assertion that there is no one "American" childhood and that "every aspect of childhood is shaped by class, ethnicity, gender, geography, religion, and historical era." Childhood is a "life stage whose contours are shaped by a particular time and place. Childrearing practices, schooling, [. . .] all are products of particular social and cultural circumstances."[38] Childhood is and has been historically an evolving social construct, where few children were actually protected from social, political, or economic circumstances.[39] For African American children in particular, the coupling of child development science about brain and intellect maturation and the racial limits of childhood "innocence" meant and continue to mean that young black people were perceived, and portrayed, as both "nonchildlike" and "invulnerable." Still, historian Robin Bernstein reminds us that young people themselves were (and are) "agential experts" on their own cultures.[40]

Recently, scholars like Bernstein have made valuable contributions to our understandings of black young people's subjectivity and the ways in which young people who lived within racially segregated spaces of the early twentieth century contended with both the violence of white supremacy and black middle-class notions of suitable behavior. Their examination of archival materials, which bring into relief the thoughts and experiences, "passions and [semi] private thoughts" of black young people, maintains not only that these exist but that childhood is "not a fixed category," as the literature bears out: childhood is a "constructed . . . stage of life" and a "constantly shifting" category; and that race, space, gender, class, and age have all "served to undermine access" to the category of childhood.[41]

Black sociologist and Howard University professor E. Franklin Frazier saw and portrayed many of the young people interviewed for his study *Negro Youth at the Crossways: Their Personality Development in the Middle States* as in need of rehabilitation, relief, and release from the confines of Jim Crow racial segregation.[42] But young people's "interactions with institutions, social science research, media, and educational bodies created an alternative archive that provides a steady backbone for research [on black youth]," as Marcia Chatelain makes clear.[43] In reading these archives and contemporary ethnographic research, girlhood studies' scholars mobilize feminist theory to argue that, despite marginalization, girls "find strategies to play important roles in their respective communities and cultures"; "exercise their own will and personal choices"; and "serve important symbolic functions" in society.[44] Fisk University's black sociologist Charles S. Johnson interviewed African American young people for his book in the same American Youth Commission series for which Frazier conducted his DC research.[45] Susan Cahn's *Sexual Reckonings* used Johnson's materials to focus on girls as historical actors, identifying childhood history as both political and social terrain and taking young people's lives and voices seriously.[46] Finally, Saidiya Hartman's *Wayward Lives* pushes at the "limits of the case file." Hartman narrates the lives of photographed and anonymous black girls and young women, "deemed unfit for history and destined to be minor figures," identifying them instead as "social visionaries, radical thinkers, and innovators," insistent on imagining future lives and future worlds.[47]

The above methodologies for reading and interpretation are central to this book. *Coming of Age in Jim Crow DC* foregrounds how some young people acted against the maybe imposed and expected silences of "dissemblance."[48] Young people interviewed for Frazier's adolescent personality development research project were "eager to talk" to their interviewers, partly because they might have had a history with their interviewers from participation in programs at DC's Southwest Settlement House or, in some cases, they might have been "feeling," as Cahn says, "that the very interview process itself bestowed them with some great importance." Furthermore, they had little reason to fully lie, since young people often "found support for their beliefs and practices among friends, some family members, and at least a portion of the surrounding community."[49]

Poor and working-class young people's articulations of their epistemologies, their ways of knowing and seeing both themselves and the world around them, help us to reimagine black communities in early twentieth-century urban enclaves. *Coming of Age in Jim Crow DC* offers an examination of black young people's thoughts, speech, and movement in the racially segregated US capital, as, in Hartman's words, "acts of collaboration and improvisation that unfold within [a] space of enclosure."[50] This helps us, in the contemporary moment, to see young urban black people as possessive of an inner life, an intellectual life, and interiority generally, in contrast to ways in which young people have been and continue to be portrayed by researchers, youth service professionals, policy makers, law enforcement, and the media.

The Sources

Middle-class race reform work, the revolutions in scientism, and the professionalization of the social sciences share a historical moment.[51] Uplift ideology adopted a sociological component that was promoted by the University of Chicago and subsequently by Fisk, Atlanta University, and Howard University, all sites where black Chicago school graduates held prominent positions, and resulted in a "profusion of records."[52] (I'll have more to say about this in the first chapter.) In Washington, DC, black sociologists William H. Jones and E. Franklin Frazier, each head of the Howard University Sociology Department, respectively, in the 1920s and 1930s, conducted and supervised several projects in DC's black poor and working-class neighborhoods. Jones's two research publications on housing and recreation in the wake of the 1919 riot in Washington, DC, and Frazier's study on black families and adolescent personality development form the archives at the heart of *Coming of Age in Jim Crow DC*.[53] These are supplemented by reports, public policy papers, and master's and dissertation theses produced by local white graduate students, mostly women, completing requirements for sociology degrees at Catholic and George Washington Universities, as well as census data and newspaper accounts.[54]

Frazier's adolescent research project yielded over 200 interviews with youth and their family and community members.[55] Staff for the study were mostly "young colored men and women who had completed college and had some graduate training in addition to experience in interviewing."[56] These included Laura Lee, Ruth Bittler, Thomas E. Davis, Dennis D. Nelson, Lauretta Wallace, Isadore Miles, Jean P. Westmoreland, John C. Alston, and Bernice Reed, whose brief biographies are introduced in the next chapter. Many were not that much older than the young people they would interview and in some cases much younger than the parents and community members. Some hailed from local black middle-class families and had worked at local black social service and cultural institutions, so they often had preexisting relationships with some of the young people they interviewed.

Young people were selected through their membership in Frazier's list of "Boy and Girl Scout troops, dramatic, social and recreational clubs connected with settlement houses, the Y.M.C.A. and Y.W.C.A.; groups of upper class youths in high schools; a group of delinquents, a group of domestic workers, and a club from a Baptist Sunday School. A small number of youth were picked up at random on the playgrounds and on the streets."[57]

Frazier's methodological approach required his research assistants to "memorize the guided interview outline and to make trial interviews which were then discussed with [him] before they entered upon the regular field work," although it is unclear from the transcripts whether interviewers actually adhered to this protocol.[58] Frazier's instructions included the following directives:

> We want to find out what these adolescents are feeling, are thinking, and are doing because of the fact that they are members of a minority group. . . . A personality document ought to be at least 30 typewritten pages when it is completed. [So] this may take three or four interviews. However, you will have a picture of the boy, that is how he looks, how he feels, how he thinks and how he acts. Of course, this would involve some information on his family, that is his relationship to his parents and brothers and sisters in the past and during the present time.[59]

This design yielded, in some cases, long transcripts of interviews with different members of black DC's poor and working-class communities.

Working with these materials presented a methodological challenge. How does one produce a historical narrative that focuses on the lived experiences and inner lives of poor and working-class African Americans without falling into the "pitfalls" of pathology, as W. E. B. Du Bois did in his examination of Philadelphia's Seventh Ward, and as Frazier did in his studies of black family formation?[60] How can subjectivity and personal ideologies, then, be discerned from this archival material? Thinking about Zora Neale Hurston's experiences with resistance in her ethnographic research, and Darlene Clark Hine's culture of dissemblance, black women's intentional practice of hiding private feelings from public exposure, my challenge was to look at young people's answers as possible gaming or performance, or both, while also analyzing the ways that the construction of those answers gestured toward ideology and self-knowledge.[61] No doubt individuals did not share indiscriminately or arbitrarily, and their answers were certainly constrained by the questions they were asked.

These interviews were produced at the same moment that the Works Progress Administration (WPA) was conducting interviews with formerly enslaved people, but they differ significantly in both process and content from the WPA narratives. While the WPA narratives have been a source of contention for historians, in terms of accuracy and ethics, for Frazier's interview subjects less time had passed between the experiences about which individuals were being asked, and, maybe more importantly, researchers who conducted many of the interviews with young people were mostly young African Americans themselves, albeit from a different socioeconomic background than their subjects. Their age and racial identities may have allowed for the development of some level of trust or comfort in the process. Furthermore, interviews generally were conducted over the course of one or two years and many interviewers had previous relationships with some of the young people, so that time and familiarity may also help to make the sources more reliable for accessing interviewees' interiority.

While interviewers asked questions that often sought to reinscribe tropes about black working-class communities—ones that classified particular cultural productions as raced, gendered, and classed—sometimes subjects provided answers that reinforced these and other times they did not. Sometimes they answered a question they had not even been asked and took the opportunity to tell stories of themselves and their histories. Other times, they discussed ideas that interviewers were not expecting and which were not ultimately used in the official publications or reports. My eye became trained on these moments of thoughtfulness and introspection, of engagement, of inflection, and of tangents, obfuscation, and deflection.

While the interviews of family and community members were left in transcript form, Frazier and his research assistants literally cut up youth interviews and retyped sections onto large notecards into thematic subject areas, such as "recreation," "gangs," "religious participation," "interracial interactions." These notecards were detached from an individual's other answers, from descriptions of neighborhood and family, detached even from a person's name, coded so they were anonymous. Some no-

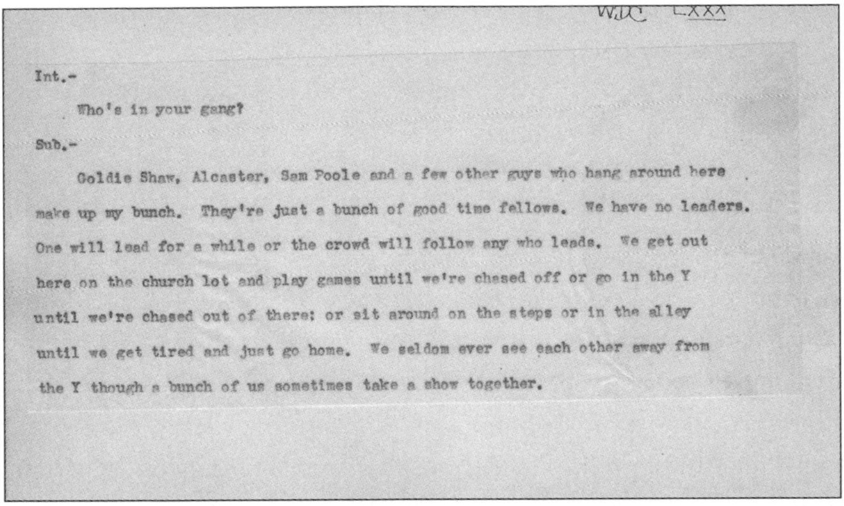
W.D.C. LXXX

Int.-

Who's in your gang?

Sub.-

Goldie Shaw, Alcaster, Sam Poole and a few other guys who hang around here make up my bunch. They're just a bunch of good time fellows. We have no leaders. One will lead for a while or the crowd will follow any who leads. We get out here on the church lot and play games until we're chased off or go in the Y until we're chased out of there: or sit around on the steps or in the alley until we get tired and just go home. We seldom ever see each other away from the Y though a bunch of us sometimes take a show together.

Figure I.1. Notecard from Frazier study. E. Franklin Frazier Papers, research study for Negro Youth at the Crossways, Moorland–Spingarn Research Center, Howard University.

tecards and some transcripts of interviews included the questions asked and responses or reactions by interviewers, while others included merely the answers with a hint of what the questions might have been. I began with this pile and a master list of young people, separated by sex, their addresses, and their "socio economic class," as determined by Frazier.

In an effort to not reinscribe the artificial categories Frazier created, I pieced together the coded notecards to get a sense of both the fuller interview and the fullness of the person interviewed: the ways in which their answers flowed one to the other; what information they shared unsolicited; questions they may have had for the interviewer; and ways in which trends in their answers tell us something: give us a hint of their ideological frameworks, their core beliefs at that moment. The process included a reassembling of interviews, finding the community and family member interviews with which they matched, and reading them as a collection of a particular family and community. Using census data,

Frazier's collected data, contemporary maps, and DC newspapers, I crafted narratives that place young people socially, temporally, and spatially within their city, drawing out ideas, philosophies, reactions to Jim Crow, and articulated visions of the future.

A few young people stand out in the archival materials. It is unclear why so much of their interviews remain. But the following chapters are centered around these larger interview sources: Southwest's seventeen-year-old Myron Ross Jr. and fourteen-year-old Susie Morgan. These young people's extensive interviews bring into relief the realities of their dynamic inner lives. Specifically, Myron and Susie ably, eloquently at times, articulate complex notions of burgeoning sexuality, gender, and racial identities; political consciousness; and internal contradictions about violence, crime, leisure, and education. All of this stands in stark contrast to the idea that young black urban people were/are not capable developmentally and otherwise of being engaged in cultivating intellectual theorizations about the worlds in which they live, and that specifically black urban youth were politically apathetic to the worlds around them.

Coming of Age in Jim Crow DC begins with a look at the politics of black adolescent personality development and focuses on how the archival materials that form the basis for this study came to be. Chapter 1, "A Chronic Patient for the Sociological Clinic," centers on Howard University's Sociology Department, the axis out of which came a number of research projects on African Americans in Washington, DC, during the New Negro era. Sponsored by the American Youth Commission (AYC) and funded by the Rockefeller Foundation, black sociologists William Henry Jones and E. Franklin Frazier took an interdisciplinary social scientific approach to their research in an effort to understand inter-racial relations and prevent racially motivated violence. They examined poverty, juvenile delinquency, and race relations—issues they saw as the result of black migration to and the growth of the black population in Washington, DC. The chapter situates their research within larger ideological and methodological movements for professionalization in the burgeoning social sciences of sociology, anthropology, and psychology and psychiatry. The reader may choose to come back to this chapter out of order so as to dive into the rich narratives in the following chapters.

Chapter 2, "Course We Know We Ain't Got No Business There, but That's Why We Go In," examines the racialized space and spatialized race of the small urban capital as the growing federal presence expanded into predominantly and historically black and poor areas of the city. The turn-of-the-century City Beautiful movement intended to make Washington, DC, both a new imperial capital and an attractive place for tourists and government workers alike. As the Federal Triangle expanded, imposing itself on the historically black and predominantly poor Southwest neighborhood, city planners, over the course of the next forty years, threatened to redevelop these communities, so that displacement was always imminent for many black poor and working families. This chapter examines how African American young people perceived and negotiated the capital city's multiple geographies of race, class, and gender, reshaping the spatial conditions of their lives. Young people articulated racial identities based in the social and "spatial meanings of power" inherent in the contrast of the symbolism of Washington, DC, and its Jim Crowed realities.[62]

The second section of the book follows these mostly first-generation urban teens as they grapple with the new economic, social, and political realities of the District. Because of the roles that young people have been assigned in the so-called pathological urban black family, the third chapter, "I Would Carry a Sign," spotlights young people's complicated political ideas and identities, specifically how they understood and negotiated Jim Crow's political manifestations in their daily lives, as well as their positions on local and national social justice campaigns. Next, chapter 4, "Right Tight, Right Unruly," amplifies young people's voices as they articulate imaginings for their futures and experiences with their sexual, racial, and gender identities in formation. It brings into relief their complex notions of leisure, recreation, and "fun." For some, their free time included individual, sexual, and gang violence, even as these same young people were alternately involved in supervised and sanctioned recreational sports and hobbies.

Taken together, *Coming of Age in Jim Crow DC*'s sources, methodology, and narratives speak out beyond W. E. B. Du Bois's "veil," the barrier to full engagement, with the structures of white supremacy at its heart.[63] Poor and working-class young black people frequently show up in social science as statistics: nameless, faceless, and voiceless, rendered only in the aggregate as an urban monolith. *Coming of Age in Jim Crow DC* removes often-invisible ordinary black young people from their sociological frames, a lens through which they were (and continue to be) viewed as pathological and deviant, and places them instead within their own contexts. This project begins at the mundane, the sometimes beautiful, sometimes ugly, always complex and messy quotidian experiences and thoughts, centering the articulations of average black young people who were migrants to or long-term residents of the physically and symbolically changing nation's capital during hard economic times.

The young people within these pages were not members of DC's black aristocracy. Yet they too were DC New Negroes, part of a movement of artists, activists, and intellectuals. They cultivated and mobilized analytic philosophies, and articulated experiences with urban modernity that become audible *through* the very discourse of social science. Young people spoke critically and with mastery about the incongruent juxtapositions of Washington, DC, invoking history and practicing a politics of mobility, claiming their right to the city and reterritorializing spaces.[64] In contrast to the ways they were portrayed, we come to understand that young black poor and working-class people had complex social and intellectual lives in which they conceptualized for themselves and made sense of family, work, play, desire and sexuality, racial segregation, violence and criminality, respectable behavior, community responsibilities, and the possibilities for the future, especially important in the contested spaces of Washington, DC. For many of these young people, the larger racial and cultural renaissance and early political and civil rights campaigns were sometimes mere backdrops to their already sufficiently full and necessarily dynamic inner, everyday lives.

Finally, I have kept all the names of the young people interviewed intact. I hope that descendants of the folks that appear in these narratives will find pride in their ancestors and be as inspired hearing these voices as I was when I happened upon them in the belly of Howard's Founders Library.

Figure 1.1. "Dingman Place, Negro Tenements." Marion Post Wolcott, photographer. Farm Security Administration, September 1941. Library of Congress, Prints & Photographs Division, FSA/OWI Collection [LC-USF34–090005-D].

1

"A Chronic Patient for the Sociological Clinic"

Interdisciplinarity and the Production of an Archive¹

The Negro problem was in my mind a matter of systematic investigation and intelligent understanding. The world was thinking wrong about race, because it did not know. The ultimate evil was stupidity. The cure for it was knowledge based on scientific investigation. [. . .] Whites said, Why study the obvious? Blacks said, Are we animals to be dissected and by an unknown Negro at that? [*The Philadelphia Negro*] was as complete a scientific study and answer as could have been given [. . .]. It revealed the Negro group as a symptom, not a cause; as a striving, palpating group, and not an inert, sick body of crime; as a long historic development and not a transient occurrence.

—W. E. B. Du Bois, "Science and Empire," *Dusk of Dawn* (1940)²

E. Franklin Frazier joined Howard University in Washington, DC, as head of the Sociology Department in 1934. Frazier was part of a core group of New Negro intellectuals brought in by Howard's first black president, Mordecai Johnson. Johnson, who came to Howard in 1926, was determined to help further position Howard at the nexus of New Negro knowledge production, hiring, in addition to Frazier, Alain Locke in philosophy, Rayford Logan in history, Charles Drew in Howard's College of Medicine, Ralph Bunche in political science, Abram Harris in economics, and Charles Hamilton Houston in the School of Law.³ Frazier, born just across the border in Maryland, had been an undergraduate at Howard, having received from his black Baltimore high school the annual scholarship to attend the preeminent university. By 1930, he had completed his PhD at the Chicago school of sociology, thought of as the leading site for sociological training in the US, and had been a Russell Sage fellow at Columbia University in New York City.[4] Frazier had also, by this time, developed a close mentor relationship with W. E. B. Du Bois, who tried to advocate for Frazier when he had been forced to leave Atlanta University for his 1927 publication of what was to some a controversial essay, "The Pathology of Race Prejudice."[5] Frazier's work built on what Du Bois outlined in the above quote about his 1899 research project *The Philadelphia Negro*, that of the mobilization of "scientific investigation" to correct notions of racial inferiority, and a paradigmatic shift away from a biological causation theory of what were identified as "racial" differences in the United States.[6]

E. Franklin Frazier was heir to Du Bois's turn-of-the-century innovations in empirical research. Just as Frazier was publishing his most influential work, *The Negro Family in the United States* (1939), Du Bois reflected on the ways in which *The Philadelphia Negro* "revealed" what he saw as an essential truth: poverty in black communities had a historical and structural causation; long-term environmental factors of racial and economic discriminatory policies were to blame.[7] Du Bois's methodological approach heralded a general move in sociology that, according to one scholar, "sought to shed its ties to moral philosophy" and rather "presented an 'objective' picture of society."[8] *The Philadelphia Negro* sought to disavow race as a biological concept by proving the structural and historical causations of poverty, demonstrating the impact of a history of racial and economic discrimination on African Americans. Du Bois hoped, as did other black reformers and an emerging group of black social scientists, Frazier included, that the professionalization of social science fields would help legitimize remedies for and theories about black poverty, licentiousness, and crime.[9] Despite the ways in which Frazier's work was later used to advance a "culture of poverty" thesis, Frazier's research, like Du Bois's earlier studies, sought to make a structural argument rooted in Jim Crow racial segregation for the ways he found black culture, and specifically poor and working-class black culture, to be deficient.[10]

Just as he was putting the final touches on *Negro Family in the U.S.*, Frazier embarked on a two-year research project for the American Youth Commission. The AYC was part of the American Council on Education, a federal agency privately funded by the Rockefeller Foundation. In 1937, the AYC "selected" for a "special Negro study" the "problem" question of "What are the Effects, if any, Upon the Personality Development of Negro Youth of their Membership in a Minority Racial Group?"[11] The national study aimed to "emphasize new ways of looking at race relations." Despite Du Bois's early interventions, and even the Chicago school's and Franz Boas's turn to culturalist explanations for differences among people, AYC project supervisor and sociologist Robert L. Sutherland wanted the study to *straddle* a "middle position between race as a biological [and race as] a social fact."[12]

Frazier's resulting publication, *Negro Youth at the Crossways: Their Personality Development in the Middle States*, would engage many of the concepts that became better known in *The Negro Family in the United States* and on which Gunnar Myrdal's 1944 *An American Dilemma* would build.[13] *Negro Youth* sought to "determine what kind of person a Negro youth [was]." The study aimed to examine the psychological impact of Jim Crow discrimination on black adolescent "personality development."[14] It was part of a series of publications that included sociologist Ira De Augustine Reid's 1940 *In A Minor Key: Negro Youth in Story and Fact*; anthropologist (William Boyd) Allison Davis and psychologist John Dollard's *Children of Bondage*, originally titled *American Children of Caste* (1940); anthropologist William Lloyd Warner's *Color and Human Nature: Negro Personality Development in a Northern City* (1941); and Charles S. Johnson's *Growing Up in the Black Belt: Negro Youth in the Rural South* (1941).[15]

The studies emphasized links between black family structures, class, and what Frazier would define as both cultural and psychological "pathologies," albeit temporary and mostly environmentally caused.[16] Young people were especially vulnerable to social forces that included family, community, school, and religious institutions. In the study, Frazier sought "to determine what kind of person a Negro youth is or is in the process of becoming as a result of the limitations . . . placed upon his or her participation in the life of the communities in [DC]."[17] He aimed to advocate for the end of racial segregation (and ultimately racial prejudice), arguing that "the class structure of the Negro community" significantly influenced family, community, school, and religious institutions.[18] He posited that Jim Crow restrictions had a worse impact on black poor and working-class young people, producing feelings of inferiority and ultimately antisocial behaviors. Still, he maintained the straddle laid out by the project's director, defining personality as being a product of both "biological inheritance" *and* "social experience."[19]

This focus on youth was partly a result of the early twentieth-century emergence of "child science" in a number of disciplines, including social work, psychology, and psychiatry. The Progressive Era federal Children's Bureau in DC launched a number of programs and produced a number of advice manuals on childrearing and education. The Depression ushered in renewed interest in the nuclear family, but many young white people were delaying marriage until their economic circumstances improved and instead engaging in premarital sex. Young people's abilities to participate in recreational activities were also severely curtailed, so young white men were spending more time "hanging around corners, creating mischief, and in general hell-raising to break the monotony of their daily lives." Young white girls and women were reading "cheap magazines."[20]

While juvenile delinquency had become seen as environmental, child science experts proposed medical and psychological treatment, including "mental hygiene" clinics and a visiting teacher program, rather than addressing structural socioeconomic inequities. Most of these services, however, were not readily available to poor and working-class African American young people.[21] Just as the new juvenile justice system was professionalizing, black juvenile delinquency was being highly monitored, and programs and policies were crafted around it. While some police forces around the country were "embrac[ing] new models of social welfare-minded friendliness [toward] children," these children were seldom immigrants, or black migrants, or poor and working-class African American long-term residents.[22] Despite a cultural shift in thinking and a recognition of the structural realities brought to bear by economic crisis on white youth, social science and psychiatry persisted in attempting to understand the cultural and behavioral "pathologies" of poor and working-class black youth.

Even with the equivocation required by the AYC, Frazier and his generation of New Negro intellectuals welcomed the pivot away from concepts about racial inferiority as a biological fact.[23] By the time Frazier arrived at Howard University in the mid-1930s, Howard was already the center of New Negro intellectual life. Philosopher Alain Locke had become the head of Howard's Philosophy Department in 1921 and would soon after edit the *Survey Graphic*'s "Harlem: Mecca of the New Negro" and publish his subsequent anthology, *The New Negro: An Interpretation*.[24] As the title of this chapter reflects, Locke's *Survey Graphic* essay "Enter the New Negro" celebrated this new direction in the social scientific study of black life. Locke posited that because of "intellectual" advances and a renewed "keen curiosity," "the Negro [was] being carefully studied, not just talked about and discussed." Along with other New Negro intelligentsia, Locke lauded the "new objective and scientific appraisal" "rather than the old sentimental interest," believing it heralded an opportunity for both "cultural exchange and enlightenment," and an "era of critical change."[25]

Though Locke insisted that this "new negro" was no "social ward or minor," and could no longer be portrayed as "the sick man of American Democracy," the interwar period saw renewed social science interest in black poor and working-class communities. In the wake of the racial violence of summer 1919, researchers and reformers became invested in "the study of race relations" as a way to identify ways to prevent future conflicts.[26] The Great Depression also enhanced the economic crises and discrimination affecting the large portion of African Americans already living in poverty in the capital. New Deal programs, as has been assessed by historians since and as had been assessed contemporarily by many local black reformers and political activists, often did not address the needs of the most vulnerable African Americans.[27] While many inter-war reformers and social scientists, like Du Bois before them, identified policy and structural inequities, they continued to research these communities looking for answers to poverty, health disparities, behaviors deemed as culturally distinct, and ways to prevent racial tensions.

Sometime after Locke came to Howard, Frazier's predecessor in sociology, William Henry Jones, mobilized the university's resources to conduct two research projects in the wake of the DC 1919 Red Summer. In 1925, Jones was called on to conduct a twenty-six-month survey, the goal of which was "to discover some of the social forces and factors which [were] powerful determinants of the cultural aspects of Negro life in Washington." Funded in part by one of the many iterations of the Washington Interracial Committee, organized after the 1919 riot, and at the behest of the Juvenile Protective Association of D.C., a Progressive Era social welfare agency, Jones, with the help of students from his "Social Pathology" class, researched and then published *Recreation and Amusement among Negroes in Washington, D.C.*[28]

In the study, Jones identified both acceptable and "pathological" forms of recreation, which "demoralized" the community.[29] The research revealed the new interest in urban leisure and recreation tied to black migration in the interwar era. Its findings suggested a causal relationship between inadequate appropriate options for the use of idle time and racial violence. Jones found that "the routinized life [of an urban center], along with mechanical and impersonal relationships, produce[d] a great deal of social unrest and stress." City dwellers required "relaxation and relief from intense psychic and muscular application." But for black migrants in particular, the city needed to "control and conserve play," in order for them not to seek "relief [in] the old and more deeply rooted racial habits."[30]

Two years later, Jones published *The Housing of Negroes in Washington, D.C.: A Study in Human Ecology* where he stated that the 1919 riot had "resulted from the effects of a rather heavy influx of Negroes from the South into the National Capital during the period of the Great War."[31] This "heavy influx" also gave rise to a number of other residential problems, according to Jones: overcrowding and "congestion" of African Americans in small, often alley, areas, breeding vice and immorality, isolation, disease, and general cultural "retardation"; the "invasion" of black folks into white neighborhoods resulted in whites moving out if they could or organizing strategies to prevent incursion in the form of violence and covenants; and the creation of geographic (and mostly segregated) communities that faced racial discrimination and prejudicial treatment.[32] DC's racial segregation, indicted by Jones, was just one part of how racism manifested in the capital: the 1920s represented the height of Ku Klux Klan activity. The local chapter's baseball team called itself "an auxiliary to the police department," and held marches along Pennsylvania Avenue in the summers of 1925 and 1926, despite protests from both the NAACP and local Jewish groups.[33] This atmosphere made the work of New Negro researchers and reformers critical.

Jones's investigations were part of not just the movement away from theories of biological determinism to theories of cultural adaptation in the social sciences, but also a move toward interdisciplinarity in social science research, and an emerging partnership between private and public agencies subsidizing projects. Many social scientists adopted an assimilationist model that theorized about the integration of, in Jones's case, African American migrants in urban and industrial areas. New empirical methodologies that "abandon[ed] biology and mobiliz[ed] the concept of culture" were used to inform social reform and mitigate the Progressive Era's modernization process. But also by the interwar period, many thought that this new empiricism could yield solutions for managing social problems, like racial conflict in urban areas, for example.[34] The turn to scientism that Du Bois had heralded manifested in the Progressive and interwar eras' community studies, which focused on "race, the city, empirical methods, and cultural contacts," supported by theories of social organization coming out of the Chicago school of sociology at the University of Chicago under the leadership of Robert Park and Ernest Burgess.[35]

Jones's introductory remarks in *Recreation and Amusement* centered the importance of urban "social organization" and "social activities" for black migrants, arguing that organized leisure and recreation facilitated and hastened black migrant "assimilation" and "adjustment to urban life."[36] In the study on housing two years later, Jones's recommendations, presented at the end of the book, focused mostly on structural and institutional remedies. He recommended to Congress that the inhabited alleys of Washington be "eliminated" and turned into "minor streets and parking spaces" or "demolished" altogether. He also asked for legislation that would "provide for a more adequate" District of Columbia Health Department. To the Interracial Committee for whom he did the study, Jones recommended that they, with the help of the Washington Council of Social Agencies, "appoint a 'Standing Committee on Negro Housing'" that would work to prevent "the exploitation of Negro home buyers and renters"; drum up interest among "suitable agencies in the building of model Negro homes"; and "act as an advisory agency to prospective Negro tenants or purchasers much as the Legal Aid Society acts as the attorney or adviser of poor clients." He also made recommendations to white real estate agents and the Real Estate Board; black and white property renters; social agencies; and white builders of black housing. Some recommendations were admonitions for keeping rental rates and housing costs at "reasonable prices"; keeping property "in good repair"; entreaties against violence and other "lawless practices in dealing with Negro invasions" into white neighborhoods; and against using cheap building materials in the making of black homes.[37] Thus, Jones identified the ways in which both legal and customary obstacles were to blame

for poor and inadequate housing and its accompanying health disparities for black folks in Washington, DC.

Jones's investigations also focused on "behaviorism" and a multidisciplinary approach in examining "race relations."[38] The studies stressed
"human behavior and external physical characteristics." "To the sociologists," Jones said, "behavior and forms of interstimulation are of vastly
greater importance than the physical aspects of institutions."[39] "Behaviorism," an interwar psychological concept adopted by many disciplines,
sought to understand "the capacity of the people" to fully participate
in society in a period of "mass migration, expanding enfranchisement,
economic depression, authoritarian movements, totalitarian states, and
world war."[40] Behaviorism became central to the theoretical approach
advocated by the Rockefeller Foundation–funded Social Science Research Council.

Founded in 1923 and headed by political scientist Charles Merriam,
the Social Science Research Council was one of the growing number
of organizations supported by a private philanthropic community that
included the Rosenwald Fund and the Russell Sage, Carnegie, and
Harmon Foundations. Many foundation managers were trained social
scientists who believed that the production of scientific knowledge, in
time, would, "in the hands of competent technicians [, . . .] result in sub-
stantial *social control*," specifically of poor and working-class people.[41]

Funding bodies like the national and private Social Science Research
Council, the federal American Youth Commission, and the local DC Interracial Committee encouraged a multidisciplinary research agenda by
funding certain projects. Disciplinary boundaries were seen as obstacles
to finding viable solutions to society's problems, to understanding and
adjudicating race relations, and to producing knowledge on migrant and
other worker adaptations to newly industrialized labor and spaces. For
example, diverse groups of researchers received funding from the Laura
Spelman Rockefeller Memorial Fund to produce scientific findings and
social reform policy that centered child research in physical growth, psychology, and the "relationship between IQ and environment."[42] The se-

ries of studies of which Frazier's *Negro Youth at the Crossways* was a part brought together experts from anthropology, sociology, and psychology and psychiatry to produce a national "case study" and make recommendations for "changing stereotypes, education, social work, organized religion" *and* "lower-class standards."[43]

Frazier's *Negro Youth* and Charles S. Johnson's *Growing Up in the Black Belt* shared the time of premier psychiatrist Harry Stack Sullivan, who had formed, with cultural anthropologist Edward Sapir, the William Alanson White Psychiatric Foundation, and became known for being at the forefront of "the fusion of psychiatry and social science."[44] Johnson, in his memorial address for Sullivan, credited him with moving psychiatry out of a purely biological realm. He posited that Sullivan's emphasis on the interpersonal kept "to much of what [was] good in the biology of higher organisms, and along with this, much of what [was] good in the social psychology of the human young, in cultural anthropology and in linguistics, epistemology, ecology, social geography, political science and administration."[45]

Studies like those of Jones, Frazier, and other Howard social scientists were being used in NAACP legal briefs as evidence that "segregation was deleterious to African Americans."[46] Walter White, the NAACP's executive director during the 1930s, penned *Rope and Faggot: A Biography of Judge Lynch* (1929), employing "ethnography, statistics, psychology, and history to level a terse indictment" of lynching. The NAACP gained considerable support, including from President Franklin D. Roosevelt, for an antilynching bill during the 1930s, but was not able to get it beyond the Senate floor.[47]

Not just Howard University faculty, but DC's social science students invaded black communities to study them. Students also utilized an interdisciplinary methodology and, in many cases, cited structural causation for conditions in those poor black DC communities. It wasn't just psychology and psychiatry; Marion Ratigan, a white sociology PhD student at Catholic University, engaged the new medical field of nutrition. Her research examined four alley neighborhoods in each quadrant of

DC. In the early twentieth century, tuberculosis had a high rate among poor and working-class black Washingtonians. But so did heart disease, hypertension, and just plain malnutrition.[48] In an effort to make a causal link between socioeconomic status, nutritional deficits, and the incidence of disease, Ratigan counted stoves, beds, iceboxes, tables, dressers, overstuffed furniture sets, pictures on the walls, victrolas, pianos, and telephones in homes. She sought to create a data set of material possessions, folks' daily diets, and their rates of disease. She found that

> people in the alleys are subject to disease—many diseases—not because they are "a" people but because they are people—people who are subject to diseases associated with their low socio-economic status, with its piteous and devious occupations, dank and unsanitary housing, scanty and threadbare clothing, unbalanced and meager diet, abridged and neglected education, unwholesome and temptation–provoking recreation, and restricted and vexatious medical facilities.[49]

Earlier, Ratigan's colleague Gladys Sellew had lived in a Northwest alley neighborhood, Union Court, just southwest of Howard University, from February 1936 until April 1938 "in as far as is possible [. . .] poverty [. . .] in order to understand [her] neighbors."[50] Like Ratigan, Sellew, who identified herself as "of the capitalistic class," having enjoyed the "comforts and luxuries of life," was completing doctoral research at Catholic University.[51] She too was an adherent of the Boasian discourse—that there were not biological determinants to racial differences, and that an interdisciplinary social scientific approach had proven that. She wrote:

> the distinction between the Negro and the white [was] not inherent, but rather a part of the culture of the present generation, influenced by slavery and the fact that the Negro has not yet been given free access to preparation for, and entrance into, the higher paid positions in industry or the higher ranks in the professional group.[52]

So Du Bois had led the way in the shift to citing structural anteced-
ents to (black) poverty and crime. Reformers and New Negro social
scientists like William Henry Jones and E. Franklin Frazier followed
suit. But the social sciences also played a crucial role in the continued
construction and reification of racialist ideologies. Both sociology and
anthropology developed alongside the eugenics movement and the rise
of social Darwinism. Despite a shift away from biological determinism, cultural practices and behaviors were still being associated with
particular "racial" groups or ethnicities, specifically those of a certain
class. While the "permanence" of biology gave way to the temporariness
of a culture transitioning through the assimilation process into modern
civilization, race as a concept organized within a hierarchy remained
consistent.[53]

Davis and Dollard's addition to the AYC series, *Children of Bondage*, stands out as an example of not only the interdisciplinary research
partnership but also the conclusions drawn that helped to reinscribe
notions of a racialized and classed black culture in need of rehabilitation. Anthropologist Allison Davis was the older brother of John Aubrey
Davis, political scientist and activist who helped to form the DC–based
New Negro Alliance (NNA), which would organize the "Don't Buy
Where You Can't Work" campaign against businesses throughout DC in
the 1930s.[54] Davis and psychologist John Dollard centered childrearing
practices in an assessment of "the racial stratification of black adolescent
personality development." Davis and Dollard brought both anthropological and psychological theories and practices to bear on their research
with black teenagers in the urban South. They posited that psychological
damage of black teens could be traced to not only social disadvantage
but also to lower-class mothers who proved to be the "instigator[s]" of
an "undisciplined, aggressive" personality type in their children.[55]

E. Franklin Frazier offered up a similar theoretical framework in his
influential work, *The Negro Family in the United States*. For Frazier, the
black family was most functional when it was "established upon an institutional basis." This meant that each member assumed their appro-

priate role as outlined by patriarchy: the father as the authority and the mother as "economic[ally] subordinated."[56] In Frazier's opinion, the most functional black families were those that had descended from free blacks. Here "family life on an institutional basis [was] highly developed, [. . . and] closely tied up with the accumulation of property" and the roles of family members.[57] He surmised that in the process of migration to the city, "family ties [were] broken, and the restraints which once held in check immoral sex conduct [lost] their force." "Social problems," Frazier posited, resulted when "rural folkways" clashed with the "legal requirements of the city," specifically those that accompanied application for "relief."[58]

While births outside marriage may have been an accepted and generally innocuous part of black southern rural culture, for Frazier once "these unmarried mothers[, often] a part of the great army of poorer migrants," moved to the city, illegitimacy became "closely tied" with family "disorganization."[59] He noted an increase in "Negro children born out of wedlock" in black families in the period after emancipation and well into the twentieth century, and made a correlation between the increase in "illegitimacy" and urban spaces. "City streets," Frazier stated, "as well as the moving picture houses, theaters, and dance halls, provide occasions for contacts which often lead to illegitimacy."[60] To be unmarried and pregnant, or to engage in premarital sexual activity, also marked a woman or girl as

> naturally [. . .] from the lower economic strata in the Negro population. As among whites, when [black] women and girls who have the advantage of education and economic security and the protection of family [became pregnant] as a result of extramarital sex relations, they [were] generally shielded both from the censure of society and from the scrutiny of social agencies.[61]

Finally, migratory men, "roving black Ulysses," and women who identified as single left children behind, and engaged in sex work in northern cities, representing "the final stages of demoralization," "debris thrown off by a bankrupt and semifeudal [. . .] South."[62]

For Frazier, without economic and cultural resources like those available to middle- and upper-class African Americans, poor black folks would "naturally" pass on the behaviors of family disorganization to their children and ultimately find themselves in "Negro communities located in the slum areas of our cities."[63] Frazier clearly identified the ways that race and class positionality influenced access, or rather lack of access, to health care and housing, as well as the ways in which they influenced public scrutiny on personal life. But he also conflated this lack of access with a necessarily natural cultural process. Thus, Frazier made a link between the development of what later social scientists would call black urban ghettos and particular southern rural migrant cultural behaviors, a culture of poverty.[64]

In *Negro Youth at the Crossways*, Frazier assigned to black poor and working-class parents an inherent inferiority and resignation caused, in his estimation, by their "southern background[s], their traditional attitudes of subordination," and lessons learned the hard way, as a result of "challeng[ing] openly the white man's authority." Examining the psychological impact of Jim Crow discrimination on black adolescent personality development, the book noted feelings among young people that included "antagonism towards whites," unfriendliness, and morosity.[65] Particular approaches to childrearing could lead to a child's "'promiscuity' in sexual relations and 'superficiality' in friendship relations."[66] Mothers imparted strategies for coping and getting along in the world, encouraging their children to "avoid conflict, ignore insults, and adopt techniques for 'getting by' [such as] 'acting like a monkey,' 'jibing,' flattery and plain lying." Thus, black mothers damaged their children's psyches and squelched self-esteem and ambition. Frazier noted that these behaviors were not evident in middle- and upper-class black households in Washington DC.[67]

Similarly, white social science students like Catholic University's Marion Ratigan and Gladys Sellew, while citing structural inequities, specifically poverty, also produced research that identified racialized cultural pathologies as inherent to poor black communities. Ratigan used language like "devious" and "unwholesome" to describe leisure and recreational activities in the poor black communities she had researched.[68] For Sellew, despite scientific advances, racial differences, even if not inherent or biological, were significant, and to some degree immutable. She blamed racialized slavery for black cultural "retardation." And while advocating for black schools to provide curricula that instilled racial pride in black children, she also found it to be "self-evident that no amount of duplication of external conditions [could] make [her] life like theirs." "I am white," she noted, "and they are Negroes." Furthermore, Sellew stated, "the concrete problems of [black] economic and *cultural social pathology* [are] determined by both *heredity* and environment" (emphasis added).[69] Another Catholic University master's student identified "illiteracy, laxity in sexual relationships, crime, vice, disease, and above all, an air of idleness" among the group of poor African American young people she studied. Dora Somerville, like Sellew, named a *culture* of poverty that manifested among black poor and working-class young people in sexually promiscuous and delinquent behaviors, even as she saw these behaviors as a result of "isolation" caused by DC's Jim Crow racial segregation policies.[70]

For both black and white social agencies, institutions, and intellectuals, poor and working-class African Americans in growing urban spaces became necessarily associated with, as Hazel Carby notes,

vice, or immoral behavior, [and] thus [. . .] could be variously situated as a threat to the progress of the race; as a threat to the establishment of a respectable urban black middle class; as a threat to congenial black and white middle-class relations; and as a threat to the formation of black masculinity in an urban environment.[71]

Much of what was theorized by social scientists in this period, New Negro ones included, is rife with underlying assumptions about what is inherent behavior, even as they attempted to disabuse the general public and governmental officials of just that. Howard's William Henry Jones and E. Franklin Frazier identified structural determinants for conditions of poverty and racial violence by shifting away from biological causation. This shift was one many black and white Progressive Era social scientists made. Frazier, and Jones before him, hoped to influence and propel social welfare policy to ameliorate economic and social conditions for poor black people in Washington, DC, invoking the significance of the District as the national capital and thus a model for the country. Frazier identified segregation and poverty as the causes of feelings of apathy and "inferiority" among "lower-class Negro youth," and for other "pathologies."[72]

Concerned about the development of a maladjusted identity among young people and the ways in which DC's restrictions informed a black young person's personality, Frazier's study included questions about sex, interracial relations, racial identity, family roles and responsibilities, local and national politics, feelings and experiences about school and with gangs, how young people spent their leisure time, and knowledge about contemporary and historical African American figures. Psychiatrist Harry Stack Sullivan not only interviewed some young people, he also administered "the Personality Inventory" test, which was designed by psychologist Robert G. Bernreuter in 1931.[73]

Over the two years of research that it took to compile the interviews for *Negro Youth at the Crossways*, Frazier budgeted some $12,000 to support himself, an administrative person, four research assistants, two of whom he delineated as "social scientists," and a "psychiatrist."[74] Thomas Edward Davis, in his late twenties during his time as Frazier's "social science analyst," was a native of Georgia and a resident of Northwest DC.[75] Davis's name can mostly be found on community observation reports and interview transcripts. Laura V. Lee was a mere twenty-one years old when she began working with Frazier on the project. Lee came highly recommended, a "Washington girl who finished high school with a good record and went to Mt. Holyoke," where she had put herself through school and thus had not been able to "[make] Phi Beta Kappa." Frazier was impressed by the recommendations and in Lee's "honor work on sharecroppers," which he called "a very excellent piece of work."[76] For the duration of the project, Lee lived in the Northwest home of her South Carolina–born parents, a railway mail clerk and a grade school teacher, along with her younger brother Richard Jr.[77] Laura Lee was charged with interviewing "lower class girls." She became very attached to fourteen-year-old Susie Morgan, and after two years of interviews she ended that aspect of their relationship, and instead became, in her estimation, more of a mentor, although she continued to document their interactions.[78]

Dennis D. Nelson, almost thirty years old, interviewed most of the boys involved in the project. Nelson was a graduate of Fisk University and had been a case worker at the Southwest Settlement House for almost a year in 1937, which meant that he had some preexisting relationships with, and thus access to, boys and their families before he began his work for *Negro Youth*. Nelson used Frazier as one of his references on his letter of inquiry, but he also came highly recommended by United States House of Representatives member Herbert S. Bigelow from Ohio, who "admire[d Nelson] as one of the finest individuals of his race."[79]

Twenty-six-year-old Jean P. Westmoreland was a native of Michigan, and while in Washington, DC, lived with her mother and aunt, both of whom had been born in North Carolina and were teachers. Noted black sociologist Ira De A. Reid laid out Westmoreland's attributes in his rather lackluster and matter-of-fact recommendation letter to Frazier: she had both a bachelor's and a master's degree, the latter received from New York University in "Educational and Vocational Guidance."[80] Westmoreland's transcripts are the only ones that often included her own reactions and comments to subjects' answers, intimating her feelings and attitudes about the lives of the folks she was interviewing.

Several others were employed for the project, about whom there is less information available. Bernice A. Reed was Frazier's student and had a master's in social work from Howard University. Lauretta J. Wallace may have been one of Frazier's oldest employees. She was in her late fifties and a graduate student in Howard's Sociology Department. John C. Alston was a part-time worker and a student of Frazier's. Thirty-seven-year-old Isadore W. Miles, who had a master's in psychology from Clark University, was also a teacher at Dunbar High School.[81] Twenty-seven-year-old New Yorker Ruth J. Bittler was Frazier's only white staff person. Bittler interviewed white union leaders and gathered data on "community race relations," having "access to the other side of the color line."[82] Finally, twenty-four-year-old Zulme S. MacNeal was secretary for the whole project, which included the research conducted in Louisville, Kentucky. Born in Louisiana, raised in Chicago, MacNeal lived in New York for the duration of the project.[83]

Interwar DC was home to the New Negro "capstone of education," Howard University. Class and color privilege positioned DC's black elite researchers and reformers to produce material that advocated for both racial uplift and racial justice, especially significant for the racially segregated nation's capital. Researchers descended upon poor black communities with their notebooks and their questions, with their observations and categorizations—sometimes they were welcomed, sometimes they were shut out. What they created and collected—interviews, surveys, studies, and reports—while attempting to impute structural and environmental forces at work, often reinforced the relationship between racialist ideologies and our understandings of poor and working-class urban black folks, specifically making a correlation between poverty and particular kinds of behavior, including criminality, violence, illegitimacy, and truancy.[84] This way of viewing urban African Americans continues to be, to borrow from Hazel Carby, "a widely shared discourse of what [is] wrong with black urban life."[85]

Contrary to the conclusions they drew, these materials also provide a window into life outside their categorizations and research agendas. During his work on *Negro Youth*, psychologist Harry Stack Sullivan was impressed by one of his subjects. He documented seventeen-year–old "Warren Wall's" capacity for serious thought, his "unquestionable durable friendships," and his "projection of personal experiences in his generalizations." Wall, the pseudonym for Southwest DC teen Myron Ross Jr., had displayed an ability, according to Sullivan, to "discriminate [Sullivan] as a person from 'the white man' as a generalized object of hostility." Myron, Sullivan noted, "took himself, his past and the problematic future with considerable and rather realistic seriousness."[86]

Seventeen-year-old Myron Ross Jr. was not the only young black person who took himself seriously. Sullivan's above assessment is evidence that interviewers, social workers, reformers, and social scientists, despite their inclinations for classification and the ways in which they were steeped in conventional race theories of the moment, sometimes noted the complexities and nuances of the personhood of their subjects. Invasion of the private lives of poor and working-class black Washingtonians by Frazier and his *Negro Youth at the Crossways* staff, and an assumption of black youth subjectivity, yielded the archives from which the subsequent narratives emerge. In spite of their harmful codifications, and maybe because of their political agendas for reform and amelioration, DC's interwar social researchers provided a forum for their mostly poor and working-class young black subjects to express opinions, beliefs, and thoughts on an array of issues including segregation, education, leisure and recreation, work, religion, sex and sexuality, gender and familial roles, and politics. And it is these musings that are at the center of the remaining chapters.

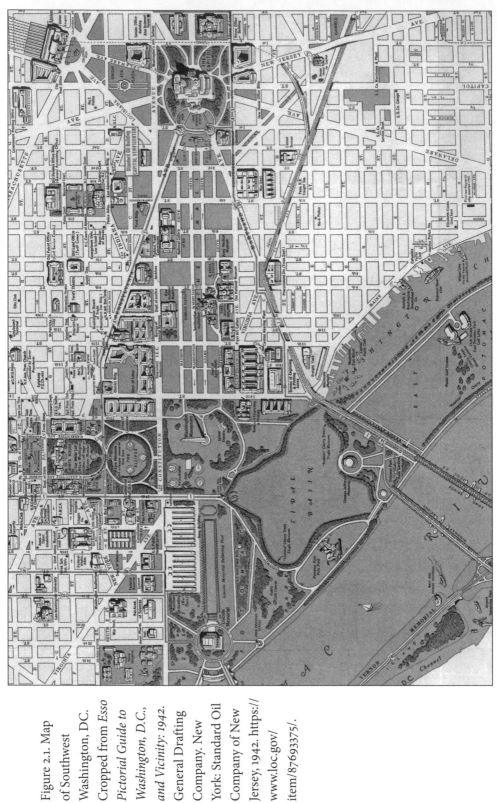

Figure 2.1. Map of Southwest Washington, DC. Cropped from *Esso Pictorial Guide to Washington, D.C., and Vicinity: 1942.* General Drafting Company. New York: Standard Oil Company of New Jersey, 1942. https://www.loc.gov/item/87693375/.

2

"Course We Know We Ain't Got No Business There, but That's Why We Go In"

Racialized Space and Spatialized Race

Walking through the Southwest area several things stand out. One is the run down condition of the buildings [. . .]. Back yards were full of junk. There were two [. . .] streets of row houses in fair condition. No other streets were in any semblance of being well kept. The general impression [. . .] was that of decay. [. . .] the general atmosphere was that associated with dire poverty.
—Ruth J. Bittler, interviewer, April 5, 1938[1]

Southwest was one of the four quadrants of Washington, DC, a poor and working-class predominantly black community with a long history as an African American enclave. It had been home to both enslaved and free African Americans in the antebellum period. In the 1850s, Southwest had housed a mission and day school, established by formerly enslaved Marylander Anthony J. Bowen who had also assisted escaped runaways to Philadelphia. In the period during and after the Civil War, newly freed people settled in the conveniently located Southwest neighborhood, with its proximity to employment at the shipyard and the gunpowder factory.[2] Southwest felt the impact of black migration to the capital city in the early twentieth century, with at least three waves between the post-Reconstruction period and the US entrance into World War II. The appeal of DC was a product of both perceived and actual employment possibilities and the possibilities for social and political equality.[3] As African American migration to the city grew, Four and a Half Street, which ran north to south through Southwest, acted as a racial dividing line, with African American migrants and longer term black residents living mostly in the blocks east of it. It was a "busy thoroughfare" of both black- and white-owned groceries and barbershops, where by the mid-1930s (white) lovers kissed in cars or openly displayed affection "all down the street."[4]

Southwest was also most vulnerable to the "city beautiful" movement to make the District of Columbia a global capital city. In the Progressive Era, DC's landscape became a canvas on which a national identity would be painted, putting Southwest and other poor black communities squarely in the crosshairs for bulldozing. DC's African American poor were seen by city planners as "the greatest drawback to the civic beauty of Washington." Their homes, often in alleys, "constitute[d] the greatest menace to real estate values in the city."[5] With the country's new international prominence in the wake of the Spanish-American War, city planners strove to bring the capital physically in line with other world capitals, to make it "the show-window of the Nation."[6] The City Beautiful movement, with its congressional backing, created a plan that included parks, parkways, federal buildings, and the monumental core we now know of as the National Mall and Federal Triangle. Designers hoped that new public spaces would work to position the capital as an "open air cathedral for American patriotism" and as "the Paris of America," simultaneously attracting tourists and engendering national pride.[7] DC's black poor and working-class communities stood in stark contrast to this vision. Lawyer and social reformer Charles Weller in his 1909 study *Neglected Neighbors: Stories of Life in the Alleys, Tenements, and Shanties of the National Capital* described these spaces as overcrowded "unwholesome hovels [and] plague spots" of disease, poverty, and vice, "nestl[ed] close beneath the window of the Capitol dome."[8]

Poor black communities, especially those in Southwest, closest to the expanding federal core, garnered more and more attention from private charities and the press. Congressional committees "complained that back alleys were filled with vicious classes of people with unclean habits over whom it was impossible to exercise proper police or sanitary regulation."[9] A 1907 Civic Center Committee annual report noted the threat to public health, saying: "These dwellings often house our servants, and a large part of the washing is done there, and thus the filth and disease germs which infest these houses are not confined to their inhabitants, but are carried into our own homes."[10] Even Jacob Riis, the photographer who was famous for pushing for the demolition of the slums in New York's Five Points neighborhood and cleaning up the city's drinking water, called DC's poor neighborhoods "worse than New York's," a "menace to civic health and breeding places of vice and crime." He warned against ignoring the problem, saying it would "spread" and the city would ultimately have to "pay the bill."[11] The Civic Center Committee issued a report that "blam[ed] congested housing conditions for both high incidences of disease and immorality, [and] claimed that inhabited alleys helped make Washington one of the most unhealthy cities in the nation." The report called the conditions "truly appalling, in view of the facts that Washington is supposed to be a modern city."[12] "These country negroes," it said, "could reach higher standards; but as it is in their hidden retreats, they dwell in a state of arrested development . . . the poor man, bound to the treadmill of daily toil, requires all the agencies that can be provided."[13]

Alleys of the early twentieth century (and generally) had a particular reputation: they were thought to be transient places, and the natural and crowded homes of new migrants to any city. And in DC, alleys were described as places with high mortality rates, incidences of disease, where "every kind of vice" could be found, including "robbery and theft," drinking, and "family disorganization [and] illegitimacy," where individuals who had "no relation" to each other lived together and single mothers who had "no idea of [marrying] soon" resided.[14] Thus, poor black migrant and native residents, not all of whom lived in alley neighborhoods, came to be seen as a blot on the landscape of the capital. By 1914, the congressionally sponsored Alley Dwelling Authority worked on a demolition and relocation scheme for many poor black neighborhoods throughout Washington, DC, but especially in Southwest.[15] Still, Southwest's imminent destruction did not seem to impact the arrival of African Americans to DC and to Southwest in particular, which in many cases was more affordable than other parts of the city.

The capital continued to be a desirable destination for African Americans from the turn of the century through World War II, despite the lack of voting rights, that there had not been a black person in Congress between 1901 and 1929, and the presence of racial violence and segregation, whether they were migrating from just next door or from further south.[16] If you were lucky, you could secure a low level janitorial, messenger, or charwoman position in the federal government. Others also came to DC to be "as near the flag" as possible, as one South Carolinian native put it.[17] DC was the "border crossing between Jim Crow" even though it was situated below the Mason-Dixon Line. It signaled the first stop on the way to the North and, for those who stayed there, the capital appeared to offer both the protection and the liberty associated with the North in particular, and with American democracy in general.[18] Domestic worker Velma Davis migrated to DC in 1916, saying about her move, "Washington wasn't the South. It's the Capital, and you had more chances for things. Jim Crow was there, but it was still not the South to us."[19]

Monument building, world wars, and national economic depression not only changed the black population of DC, they also changed the political, cultural, social, and spatial landscapes of the city.[20] Congressional decisions about physical space enhanced the symbolic meaning of the city, but coupled with an entrenchment of racial segregationist policies and practices in housing, federal jobs, and public spaces, it also set the terms for social relations.[21] The District's geography of power manifested in exclusions, expulsions, selected inclusions and access, and restricted mobility. While streetcars and public libraries were not segregated, and African Americans could watch baseball and football at Griffiths Stadium, residential housing, employment, shops, restaurants, hotels, theaters, recreational facilities, public schools, and sometimes streets were all spaces on which legal racial discrimination played out. Black Washingtonians could shop at DC's department stores, but only if they did not want to try anything on. And they could not watch fireworks from the steps of the Capitol during Independence Day celebrations.[22] In 1948, the National Committee on Segregation in the Nation's Capital referred to Washington, DC, as "the Capital of White Supremacy," saying "Washington [was] not a good salesman for . . . democracy," criticizing discriminatory practices against black and brown foreign dignitaries, and calling out racially segregationist policies that had created black "ghettoes."[23]

The irony of the juxtaposition between DC's emblematic aspirations and its racially and socially stratified geography was not lost on black Washingtonians. The "imagined landscape" of the capital's symbolic meaning and the "experienced landscape" was an important part of their everyday lives. "Geographies of experience," the ways in which individuals corporally encountered the built environment, were specific to an individual's race, class, gender, and age.[24] By the turn of the century, DC had become a nexus of black intellectual and cultural development with a growing population of black educators, activists, and thinkers, at the center of which was Howard University in Northwest.[25] But even the District's growing black elite class of doctors, lawyers, judges, social reformers, and government clerks who made their homes in the Northwest communities surrounding "the capstone of Negro education" were not immune from the limitations of Washington's segregated landscape.[26]

Mary Church Terrell, prominent educator, DC Board of Education member, and president of the National Association of Colored Women, had not only experienced racial discrimination while employed as a clerk in the federal government during World War I, she also lamented that "as a colored woman I may walk from the Capitol to the White House ravenously hungry and supplied with money to purchase a meal without finding a single restaurant in which I would be permitted to take a morsel of food, unless I were willing to sit behind a screen."[27] Black middle-class movement, even for the purposes of consumerism, was restricted in the nation's capital.[28] Additionally, housing for DC's growing black middle class was circumscribed. Ideas that black neighbors would bring down property values because of inherent criminality motivated white residents to create private restrictive racial covenants that were ultimately enforced as perfectly constitutional by DC courts in the interwar period.[29]

Black poor and working-class Southwest Washingtonians did not experience much of what Terrell described, relegated as they mostly were to neighborhoods with poor housing and inadequate services and facilities. Still, for poor and working-class African Americans, both migrants and natives, Washington, DC, with its growing federal core, its symbolic monuments to liberty and Democracy writ large, was a field of action. This chapter examines this field on two registers: individuals and/in spaces, and spaces and their relationship to people. Young people, in their fragmented interviews for E. Franklin Frazier's *Negro Youth at the Crossways*, were, borrowing from Katherine McKittrick, "geographic beings." They shared beliefs about and offered solutions to the injustices of segregation, thoughts and feelings about the inherent racial hostility of poverty, and ways they had developed to navigate its borders. They sometimes interrupted segregation in the built environment and at other times they simply found respite from it, sometimes in nonsanctioned spaces.

Young black poor and working-class people, perhaps less constrained by notions of acceptable behavior than adult black middle-class Washingtonians, had "a stake in the production of space" in the national capital.[30] They reappropriated corners, sidewalks, doorways, playgrounds, and even national monuments. But, they also took advantage of (black) public and sanctioned recreational spaces, like the Southwest Settlement House and Willow Tree Playground, the only black park in Southwest before it was razed to make room for buildings to house New Deal agencies in 1940. Through articulations of geopolitical ideologies, community identities and formation, noisemaking, and movements within and outside of the places to which they were confined, young black poor and working-class folks understood the ways in which space was both material and discursive. They expressed their "right to the city" and a larger national identity.[31] Their belonging was already intact, and especially so in the nation's capital.

Before the Beltway cut Southwest DC off from itself in the mid-1960s, seventeen-year-old James Richmond and his friends Kenneth Freeman, fifteen, and Morris Carter, nineteen, were neighbors. James and Kenneth lived just south of Morris Carter, whose father ran a black funeral home not far from the Southwest Settlement (or Community) House. James, who was known to his friends as "Hoghead," is the only person of this trio whose interview survived in the Frazier papers at Howard University, but the three of them appear under pseudonyms in the introductory chapter of *Negro Youth at the Crossways*.[32]

Described as "lolling" around the doorway to Morris's father's funeral home, "in the corner of two of the most run-down streets in the roughest neighborhood of the Southwest section of Washington, D.C.," James and Kenneth waited for Morris one summer afternoon, as they were observed and interviewed by Frazier's staff person Dennis Nelson. Morris's father was an undertaker, and Morris, who had already graduated high school, worked for him. According to Kenneth, Morris's father "let [them] hang around" and Morris was also "swell enough to share anything he own(ed)," so Kenneth and James spent most of their leisure time playing checkers there.[33] Kenneth, whose father was a janitor, had just played tennis that day, but needed a new racket and hoped that Morris would sell him his old one. As they chilled, Kenneth lamented his unemployment, his need of new shoes so he could return to school, and the poor quality of the tennis courts "at the other end of the [National] Mall." "The colored courts," he said, were "the last ones to be fixed up." There were new tennis courts in the city, but they were white only, and African Americans like Kenneth were no longer able to get permits to play there.[34]

James Richmond had tried to get a job for a year, but the only one he had been able to find would have required him to quit school, and he had decided not to do that, saying he "want[ed] to go to school as long as he [could]." James lived with his grandparents, and with his mother, who did domestic work. The family rented space in their home to a number of boarders in order to make ends meet. His overcrowded living conditions at H and First Streets meant that James was "seldom" at home and could "usually be seen walking in and out of the house with food in his hand in order that little time be lost getting back to his companions several blocks away."[35]

Morris finally joined them, saying he could hear them talking through the window and couldn't wait any longer to come out. The boys chatted, teasing each other sometimes, and talking freely with Nelson. Nelson had a preexisting relationship with the boys as he had been staff at the Southwest Settlement House, had played tennis and Ping-Pong with them there, and had taken them on camping trips. They noted that they could talk with Nelson "about things that bother[ed them]." So they conversed, sharing their desire for mobility: their desires to travel, to leave the city, where they felt hemmed in and bored. "We don't go to the beer joints and poolrooms," Kenneth shared, "so there ain't much left."[36] Moreover, the Settlement House, where they played Ping-Pong regularly, was so underresourced, with old or no recreation equipment, that Kenneth supposed they might be getting themselves into trouble if they didn't hang out at the funeral home. Despite what appeared to be Morris's relative material resources, he said he was not in a position to "take trips." He hadn't "been out of the city in years," and saw the army, and a "good war," as both a way to get out of DC and as a way for a young black man to "get a break."[37] Similarly, James saw the military as his way out of the city, either for himself or for his children, saying he would make sure his kids were "born somewhere outside of Washington," where there might be more opportunities and less antiblack racism.[38]

By both Frazier and researcher Dennis Nelson, the boys were described as "lazy" and as idle. What social reformers and the police may have considered "loitering," an indicator of, or at least a precursor to, juvenile delinquency, was actually, as expressed by James Richmond, Kenneth Freeman, and Morris Carter, the very thing that kept them safe. By socializing, playing checkers, and spending time together, the boys took advantage of the close proximity of the corner on which the Carter funeral home stood. They also took advantage as much as they could of the Southwest Settlement House, despite its limited resources, participating in sanctioned recreational activities and spaces related to school and in the city, like the designated black tennis courts.

Their Southwest peer and neighbor, seventeen-year-old Ellsworth Davis, son of a "laborer" and a "charwoman," described it this way: "in my neighborhood, you can go to the [Settlement House] or down to Randall [Recreation Center] when their center opens, [or] play on a vacant lot." But Ellsworth said that instead of going somewhere else, he sometimes hung "around his neighborhood with his friends," which included Morris Carter. "We're all neighbors," he said, "and it is natural that we stand around when we're all home." For Ellsworth, like for his friends, his containment by and in their segregated neighborhood made options like the military seem attractive. It also made the reterritorialization of the sidewalks and doorways and corners into community spaces that much more significant and necessary.[39]

Susie Morgan reappropriated spaces beyond her immediate neighborhood. She was fourteen years old in the summer of 1938.[40] Born in Maryland, Susie moved to Washington when she was two years old, accompanying her parents Oscar and Clara, and her older siblings, Joseph, Marcella, Dorothy, and Bertha. Susie and her older siblings had been born somewhere in St. Mary's County, Maryland, where their father Oscar was listed in the 1920 census as an oyster waterman, a Chesapeake Bay industry in which many of his neighbors, most of whom were also black Marylanders, were engaged.[41] While it is not clear what motivated the Morgans' move to Washington, DC, Southwest became their home. Initially they lived on K Street just west of Four and a Half Street, in close proximity to the Southwest wharves. Maybe Oscar had intended to work on the docks, hoping his skills would transfer. By 1938, though, Susie and her parents, her older unmarried siblings, five younger siblings, and a new baby sister resided on the alley behind C Street.

Clarks Court Alley was very much the way social reformers Charles Weller and later Thomas Jesse Jones described DC's alleys in the decades before the interwar period.[42] Bordered by C and D Streets to the north and south and Three and Four and a Half Streets to the east and west, it occupied the other side of a section of Four and a Half Street that housed some of Southwest's "red-light" businesses. Clarks Court Alley was situated just north of the elevated tracks of the Pennsylvania Railroad, which cut across the northern edge of Southwest just below the National Mall. It stood in the "shadow" of the federal government's physical presence, and was described by Frazier's researcher as treeless, "not well paved," replete with "shacks," lined with "piles of junk, trash, and tin cans," and "piles of fresh manure, the odor of which pervaded the air."[43] Clarks Court Alley was one of the over fifty alleys and courts, or interior streets that cut through blocks, and made Southwest known as "one of the toughest sections of the city."[44]

Susie's home, as was true for other Southwest alley communities, was in imminent danger. Four years before Susie was interviewed for Frazier's project, the Alley Dwelling Authority (ADA), established by Congress and empowered to condemn, convert, and "eliminate" DC's alley neighborhoods, had made it "unlawful to use or occupy any alley building or structure as a dwelling" after 1944.[45] Since the Authority's first iteration, some alleys had indeed been demolished. On just the other side of Clarks Court Alley, Willow Tree Alley had been turned into the black municipal recreational park Willow Tree Playground in 1913, but by the time Susie was being interviewed in 1938, the park was facing elimination to house Franklin Delano Roosevelt's Depression-era agencies: the Social Security Administration and the Railroad Retirement Board building. By 1938, the predominantly black St. Mary's Court was also in the process of being replaced with public housing, over which there was a fight between white surrounding area residents interested in living closer to the growing governmental core, the ADA, and the black-led Lincoln Civic Association, which described the ADA's plans for the redevelopment of alley neighborhoods as "driving people from shelter with no regard as to how they shall exist," and as "routing, colonizing, and depriving Negro people of homes."[46]

Susie Morgan's home in Clarks Court Alley was "a four-room shack," with two rooms downstairs that were shared by Susie, her parents, and her nine siblings, ranging in age from one to eighteen (three older siblings did not live at home), and two rooms upstairs occupied by another family. Alley buildings often did not include indoor plumbing or any sanitation amenities. This had not substantially changed by the 1930s. In the ones that may have had toilet facilities, these were often broken, and water supplies froze during the winter.[47] On the day Susie was visited in early May 1938, her front door stood ajar, showing "two beds, one double, one single, covered by army blankets, a bare uncovered floor, several suit cases under the beds, and dirty unpapered walls."[48] Susie was deeply and observably self-conscious, even ashamed of her poverty: she lied about her address, telling both the Southwest Settlement House staff and Frazier's interviewer that she lived on C Street rather than in the alley behind it, and she had tried her best to dissuade both from visiting her home. She had also been observed fidgeting with her clothes, adjusting hand-me-downs that were too big for her, "tucking in frayed edges" of her old sweater, and pulling up or "tucking into her shoes" cheap, ill-fitting socks. Susie's interviews were filled with descriptions of her oversized sweaters and clean but soiled dresses, and it included a comment that she had been spoken to about needing to take more baths.[49]

In spite of her shame and of having to endure the scrutiny of both researchers and Settlement House workers, Susie was aware of the contradictions presented by the juxtaposition of the neighboring federal government and its symbolism of freedom and equality with the geographically racialized poverty of her alley. Because of where she lived and its close proximity to federal government buildings and monuments, the fraught relationship between the imagined and built landscape of Washington, DC, and the experienced landscape was likely familiar to this Randall Junior High School student. With this stark reality in mind,

Susie moved about DC, knowing she was unwelcome in many places, but claiming, occupying, or repurposing them in some way.

Susie described one such example in her answer to a question about whether she and her friends interacted with law enforcement. She said they did. Much to the chagrin of local police, they "swam" in the Lincoln Memorial Reflecting Pool. One afternoon, they evaded the officer by swimming to the middle and then they mocked and laughed at him, insisting that Lincoln himself had given them permission to be there: "Good old Abraham, he said we could swim in his pool." When the police officer threatened to "beat" them, they goaded him, saying he would have to catch them first. Then they turned to Lincoln himself seated in his chair at one end of the Reflecting Pool and said, "Mr. Lincoln, you won't let him [referring to the police officer] bother us will you, Mr. Lincoln?" To which someone in Susie's group ventriloquized Lincoln, saying, "'No indeed, you all stay down in there an' swim 'till you git ready ta stop.'" They then all thanked Lincoln in unison. When the frustrated cop left to get help, Susie and her friends crawled out of the Reflecting Pool and ran![50]

Susie Morgan may not have known that in 1922, the year before she was born, before she and her family had even come to DC, when the Lincoln Memorial was dedicated, "distinguished and well-bred" African Americans were relegated to an all-black section, separated from the rest of the audience by a dirt road. From his seat in this section and through the mud, educator and Booker T. Washington's Tuskegee Institute successor Robert Russa Moton, who had been invited to speak at the unveiling of the monument, trudged to the speakers' platform to address the crowd.[51] Probably, though, Susie and her friends knew that white children could be found wading and sailing boats in the same pool out of which they were chased.[52]

In knowingly inserting themselves into a landscape that sought to and had already, historically, dispossessed them, Susie and her friends adapted the Reflecting Pool for their own purposes, to "swim." They, and other African American poor and working-class young people, often cited that there was no pool for them in Southwest. While African Americans were 28 percent of the city's population, the only black pool was located in Northwest at the Banneker Recreation Center, clear on the other side of the expanding National Mall. White Washingtonians, in contrast, both poor and middle class, had some nine pools and bathing beaches to choose from in the heat of the summer.[53] By invoking both slavery and its abolition, Susie and her friends asserted their natural and earned rights to Lincoln's Reflecting Pool, even speaking for and as the antislavery president literally presided over the space. In their play, they enacted their historical relationship with the actual place of the Reflecting Pool, cognizant of and mobilizing Lincoln's significance as the president in the US capital, as an advocate for African Americans generally, and as their personal advocate at this particular moment. While the federal core was literally accessible to black poor Southwest kids, these spaces, in spite of their symbolic embodiments of liberty, were designed for a public that in most ways did not include African Americans: the spaces were proximate, near, yet apart and verboten.

Susie also spent time in her old neighborhood, "down at the wharf." Her group of friends, the Union Street Sports, traveled down there to hang out. On a terrace above the street where "white people sat and ate," black kids, according to Susie, often stood below and sang. White people "would throw quarters and fifty cents down," making the children "scramble." Sometimes they took the children's photographs too. Susie insisted that she had never participated in this activity, saying she "wouldn't make no monkey of [herself]."[54] Frazier wrote about this experience in his section in *Negro Youth at the Crossways* on "lower class youth" and "neighborhood contacts." He ascribed "resentment" of "monkeying for whites" to "middle and upper class Negroes."[55] However, it was actually "lower class" Southwest alley resident Susie who expressed disdain for this behavior. Frazier left an essential part of the story out. Susie went on to describe how one day she had been "going by" and a quarter, seemingly thrown by a white person from this terrace, had "landed right in [her] pocket." So, while Susie was aware of and even deemed as beneath her this self-deprecating behavior, she also understood the "spatial meanings of power," in LaKisha Simmons's words, specifically the potential financial reward for this performance.

Afterwards, Susie said she was chased by the police and "beat[en . . .] good, [by the policeman's] hand an' with a switch," commenting that it was fortunate that the policeman had not beaten her with his club, which, she rightly recognized, could have been fatal. The policeman escorted her home and insisted that her mother punish her with another "beating." Clara Morgan promised the policeman to not just "beat 'em," but to "half kill 'em." As the policeman left, Clara Morgan gave him a "five finger salute," and once he was gone, she laughed. Susie said of her mother, "she didn't beat us." Her mother performed anger for the police. She may have seen neither the criminality nor the seriousness of her daughter's actions, and maybe even have thought that Susie had received enough punishment from her police escort. She also did not chastise Susie for venturing too far from home. Instead, Clara Morgan jokingly claimed the quarter as her own, but, Susie asserted, "it belonged to me," implying that she had somehow earned it.[56]

Susie Morgan moved nearly fearlessly about the city, claiming and reterritorializing spaces. She was an avid swimmer, not just in the Lincoln Memorial Reflecting Pool, but also swimming in the Washington Channel down by the Southwest wharves, even though it was dangerous and forbidden (a few children had already drowned there.) She consistently participated in activities at the Southwest Settlement House, and she spent many afternoons and evenings with interviewer Laura Lee and Lee's parents in their home nearly four miles away in Northwest, including requisite visits to Howard University's campus, where Lee often took the girls she interviewed.

Susie's movement throughout and outside of Southwest—from the wharves and Union Street north to Howard University and east to hang out at the Columbus Fountain at Union Station—demonstrated the ways in which Susie felt the city to be enough hers to move freely about it. She dodged interactions with the police and assessed and navigated other dangers. There were some city spaces through which Susie moved that elicited fear, and caused concerns for her interviewer, whose NW residence Susie often left late at night to get back to Southwest, via a "long ride on the street car," or more frequently by walking because she did not usually have carfare. Despite Susie's insistence on her own bravery, she traversed dicey sections of Southwest, like the railroad underpass, where she had experienced street harassment and physical endangerment.

For black girls moving about DC, mobility meant potential bodily harm: sexual harassment or assault from black and white boys and men. Many DC spaces put young women in danger. Another Southwest resident, fourteen-year-old Esther Wright, shared Susie's fears: coming home late "under the railroad crossing," she encountered "all sorts of men," some of whom, she said, "follow behind you and say things." She had learned to "just keep going," but she didn't like "com[ing] under there alone."[57] Young women navigated spaces that were "soaked in [spatial] meanings of power," even when these spaces were more traditional leisure spaces.[58]

DC's (black) newspapers were littered with stories of violence against black women, young and old, both in their homes and in public places, at the hands of police, husbands, boyfriends, and teachers. A seventeen-year-old working-class young woman, Hazel Hughes of Southeast, accused her boyfriend, Northwest resident Rama Gibson, of facilitating an opportunity for two other men to sexually assault her at the end of one of her dates with him.[59] Rama and Hazel were classmates at Northwest's Dunbar High School, which, by the 1930s, had already gotten a reputation as an elite, and elitist, black school.[60] In late January 1932, Hazel reported that Rama had taken her to a movie on U Street, the Northwest strip that was home to black businesses, black cultural venues, adjacent to black middle-class homes, and not far from Howard University.[61] From U Street, Hazel accompanied Rama south to a restaurant where he had worked tending the furnace in the heart of the growing National Mall. Rama used a key to get in and then attempted to rape Hazel. He was unsuccessful, but Hazel said that two other men showed up and both of them raped her. She told her mother that night what had happened and Rama was subsequently arrested. In Police Court, the doctor who examined Hazel reported that she had significant bruising, but by the time the case went to district court the doctor said he did not remember saying that. Rama denied all of it. Instead, he insisted that after the movie they had walked around U Street and then he had put her in a taxi home to Southeast. Ultimately, Rama was acquitted. His family had mobilized prominent friends, all federal employees like Rama's father, to testify as character witnesses on his behalf.[62] In DC's raced, gendered, and classed geography some spaces may have appeared *safe*, like U Street, a black middle-class enclave, or the National Mall. As Simmons deftly outlines, though, black young women, unlike black or white boys or even white girls, had a different "relationship and conceptualization of the city's landscape."[63]

Myron Ross Jr.'s experiences, too, show the different realities of DC's spatial meanings of power. Myron Ross Jr. had lived in Southwest all his sixteen years and had seen the community physically change. In his early childhood, he remembered his neighborhood as "practically woods." And for a long time, "white people never lived over in this section," so his contact with them had been mostly limited. Myron had only ever lived at Second Street between O and P Streets, in the home his father had inherited from his parents, but which in 1938 was heavily mortgaged. Myron's home, "a large red brick house of eight rooms," was "comfortably [but] poorly furnished." However, in comparison to some of its neighbors, it "contain[ed] modern sanitary facilities." Myron's house might have been considered large, except that Myron was the oldest son in a family of eight that included Norman (fourteen), Evelyn (thirteen), Wayland (eleven), Bernard (eight), Doris (seven), Hortense (six), Yvonne (five), and Roland (three). His home was alternatingly described in the interview transcript as "in need of repair," "noisy," "always torn up," and "disheveled," and as "bedlam," with a "mob of children" "tearing through" it.

Like Susie Morgan, Myron was embarrassed by his home, despite it being more than triple the size of Susie's two-room alley dwelling in northern Southwest. While he praised his parents' abilities to meet the family's needs on the modest income of his father's stagnated pay as one of the only black firemen in DC, he lamented the lack of space and general privacy in his home. He shared a room with his four brothers, and in the "small" room he kept his "few treasures and prize belongings" in a small "iron locker." His clothes were worn, but he tried his best not to look "shabby," especially around girls. Their abilities to travel as a family were hindered not only by the size of the family but also by the age and cost of maintenance of the family's one car.[64]

The Ross home also stood adjacent to "a large vacant tract of land that [had] recently been converted into an elaborate municipal playground for white children despite the fact that," according to interviewer Dennis Nelson, "white people [did] not live in the immediate vicinity of the playground." Hoover Field was less than a block away from Myron's house. He spent many an afternoon watching a handful of white kids playing, while "Negro children line[d] the fences wishing they could get in to play," he said. Myron questioned how, with a baseball diamond, a swimming pool, and tennis courts, "so much space [could] be used for a few boys and a great number of other boys have so little." The mere existence of Hoover Field and its close proximity caused Myron Jr. such anger that he could "bite a nail in two." He had "tried his best to get one of the white boys mad enough to fight about it," but as yet to no avail.[65]

When Frazier's white staff person, Ruth J. Bittler, interviewed Hoover Field's "Boy's Playground supervisor," she was told that "difficulty [was] often had with colored children." They stood "in gangs and beat up the white children on their way to the playground," said the white male playground staff person. Either this was an exaggeration, or Myron Jr.'s sentiments were not his alone and other black children had been more successful in goading a white kid into fighting over the space. The Boy's Playground supervisor saw nothing iniquitous about the white-only playground in the middle of the predominantly black neighborhood. He said that "the Negroes have plenty of playgrounds," and called the "gangs" instigating fights with white children "menaces." He looked forward to the government's plans to "build new buildings" in the surrounding areas of the playground. But unlike Myron Jr.'s father, who believed that as a homeowner he would somehow be a beneficiary of this urban improvement program, the white playground staff person understood that when the surrounding "houses [were] obtained and torn down" (Myron's house being one of those), he expected that "this section [would] go white and the cheap land" would encourage more white residents. The neighborhood would not "seem so much like a colored section," a section in which he was not happy to be working.[66] In contrast to Myron Jr.'s lamentation on the injustice of having the vacant lot in black Southwest turned into the white-only Hoover Field, the staff person not only did not see the injustice but he was eager to eliminate African Americans from Southwest altogether. He saw proposals for urban renewal as the solution, while Myron's father believed proposed projects for the improvement of Southwest would likely increase his property value.

Myron Jr.'s Hoover Field vexations were not the only experiences that led him to draw the conclusions he had about Jim Crow in the nation's capital. Despite having only ever lived in Southwest, Myron had had his fair share of excursions within and outside of the city, even at his young age. He visited his maternal grandparents who lived in rural Virginia; he went fishing with his friends in Maryland; he'd had a Southeast newspaper route where most of his clients were white; his assistance on his father's ham radio had led to Morse Code conversations with people in other parts of the world; and he was a member of the Boy Scouts. All of these had afforded Myron a range of geographical and cultural experiences.

Myron understood the spatial realities of race: that segregation and its attendant racism manifested in attitudes, on bodies, and in spaces; that it mattered where and who you were. His peregrinations outside of the city, like his "hikes over in Maryland for minnows," were often restrictive because "the pecks were so mean we didn't go over there more than two or three times." On one of his last fishing trips with his friends, they were hassled and run off by a group of white kids, who called them "niggers," kicked their fish back into the stream, argued with them, threatened them with rocks, and menaced them with their dog, as "half grown white men" laughed and looked on from a bridge above.[67]

Myron said that he had never tried to go "places where Negroes weren't allowed"; he had never tried "to crash where [he] wasn't wanted." He verbalized the "many crazy restrictions on Washington Negroes," which included stores that did not "cater to Negroes," like the one in which his mother had been forced to buy all of the hats she had tried on; white-only theaters; and "separate schools" with their resource disparities. Myron Jr. knew that Jim Crow was complex in DC—that blacks and whites "use[d] the same waiting rooms at the station, and the same accommodations on buses, street cars, and taxis"; that "white people" sometimes came "to our church and enjoy[ed] themselves," but that black folks did not go to "white churches unless they happen[ed] to be servants," and that they could not use the "same swimming pools or golf links," and could not eat in white restaurants, or sometimes even get served.[68]

These "segregation ideas," as Myron called them, literally colored his experience of one of his favorite activities, being a Boy Scout. In the summer of 1937, some 25,000 Boy Scouts assembled for the National Boy Scout Jamboree in the capital. The *Baltimore Afro-American* reported that 500 of the Scouts setting up their tent city on the Capitol Grounds on July 3 were black Scouts, including black southern delegations who were "Jim Crowed," compulsorily separated "from white delegates from the same states and given a special camp to themselves."[69] White "southern boy [scouts]," Myron said, were as mean as those kids over in Maryland. But the black newspaper showed images of white and black boys from Bermuda, DC, and Cincinnati eagerly trading badges, belts, and insignia with one another.[70] And Myron remembered affirming experiences with "foreign" Boy Scouts, that he had been "treated so nicely, by boys from the West and North and from foreign countries, [that] we forgot about the little nasty things the Southerners said and did."[71]

Figure 2.2. "Photonews: 25,000 Scouts from Everywhere Build Tent City in Washington, D.C., for National Jamboree." *Baltimore Afro-American*, July 10, 1937.

It was during the ten days of the Jamboree that Myron remembered one of the few times he had "want[ed] to be white." Because of the National Jamboree, African American troop members "went everywhere [white Scout troops] went—to Mt. Vernon and other places on the buses and hikes, and on all boat trips up and down the Potomac." White Scout troops, Myron vented, "had everything any boy could wish for, [they] had the freedom of the city, and enjoyed good times that even Negro Scouts couldn't enjoy here ordinarily." In scouting, Myron Jr. said, "a Negro boy is [only] *nearly* an equal" (emphasis added). He had met three boys his age from Cincinnati at the Jamboree who had made it to Eagle Scouts. He attributed his inability to rise in status as a Scout, to become the "first Negro Eagle Scout in Washington," to racial prejudice: there was no qualified black leadership in DC's segregated Scout organization.[72]

Myron's seeming desire to be white and his eagerness for a fistfight both served as evidence to E. Franklin Frazier and his psychiatrist collaborator Harry Stack Sullivan that Jim Crow segregation indeed had a negative psychological impact on young black poor and working-class people. The "isolated world of the Negro," Frazier wrote, influenced "his outlook on life as well as his hopes and ambitions."[73] Despite this assessment, what is clear from Myron Jr.'s narrative about space, both the hyperlocal one that included the lack of privacy within but general security and amenities (ham radio, aquariums, library) of his very full house, and the limitations and dangers of spaces and places outside of his home, in the city, and beyond, is Myron's deep consciousness about the complexity of Jim Crow, its inequalities, and what that meant for his relations with white people and with his black friends.

The racialized spaces of DC also informed Myron's understanding of future possibilities, as it did for Kenneth Freeman, James Richmond, and Morris Carter. Despite what was deemed as his "isolated" black world in the segregated city, Myron Jr.'s access through his father's ham radio operation, his visits to his grandparents, his fishing adventures, and his participation in the Boy Scouts afforded him a kind of cosmopolitanism that he took for granted, and which seemed to help him reconcile the inconsistencies of the built environment—the capital grounds of monuments on which the Scouts built their segregated tent city, but on which some black, brown, and white boys happily swapped belts and badges with one another; Hoover Playground for white kids only in the predominantly black neighborhood—and the experienced landscape, which included his parents' roles in church and civic organizations, his mobility within and outside the city with friends engaging in leisure activities, his paper route in white Southeast communities, and his choice to participate in the national organization of the Boy Scouts instead of "little athletic clubs in the neighborhood" or at school. These varied experiences formed both his understanding of the spatial dimensions and the structures of feeling of racial segregation and the ways those interacted with economic discrimination in Washington, DC.[74] Most notably, Myron mobilized his relationship with his interviewer Dennis Nelson and with Harry Stack Sullivan to access even more movement outside of the city—camping trips with Nelson, and college scouting trips to Hampton and Fisk as Sullivan's guest. At the end of one of his interviews, Myron Jr. said that his father had told him that "Washington [was] kinder to Negroes than cities farther south and that we actually [were] treated as well as Negroes anywhere farther north of here." Myron equivocated about whether or not he agreed with his father, saying instead he "wanted to see some other places before [he'd] say he lik[ed] Washington better." Echoing the comments from his peers at the opening of this chapter, Myron declared, "I would like to travel."

Myron Ross Jr. and Susie Morgan both lived in the contested space that was Southwest Washington, DC, among other folks who shared their socioeconomic circumstances. But poor and working-class black folks resided in the black middle-class Northwest enclave too. A 1938 radio broadcast proclaimed that elite black Washingtonians represented an example of "greater progress in . . . material advancement and in social adjustment than any similar group of Negroes anywhere in the world." Still a vast chasm existed between poor and working-class black folk and their middle-class counterparts, even if they had to live in the same segregated black community. The DC contradictions that black poor and working-class young people in these sections experienced were differently fraught—adjacent as they were to both the federal core's symbolism and the "black Broadway" and "black Wall Street" of DC's U Street.[75]

Lucy Savage was one of the poor and working-class young people who lived in Northwest. Sixteen years old, Lucy, her young son, her brother, two sisters, and her mother shared the one-room apartment on the lower level of a "rooming house" in a section of Northwest described as a black "slum," surrounded by "many fine houses and middle and professional class Negroes."[76] It was one of three places the Savages had lived in DC since their arrival from South Carolina sometime in the previous decade. When interviewer Jean Westmoreland visited the dark and dank basement apartment in July 1938, she met Lucy's mother out front and followed her into the building through the basement door and down a long dark hall. In the "general disorder" of the one-windowed room at the end of the hallway, Westmoreland described "odd pieces" of "dirty," "worn" furniture; two hardback chairs whose seats were "re-enforced with cardboard"; and a table "littered" with dirty dishes. In an alcove of the room, Lucy sat on a studio couch, "dirty and bumpy from loose springs," where she also slept with her one year old, Yudell. There was a bed that was covered with a "very dirty quilt, faded and torn." Westmoreland commented in her notes that this cellar had not been meant to be a living space. A furnace had been removed and shifted to the long hallway that led back to the small room. Plaster peeled from "bare, greasy, and unpapered" walls, and a "large exhaust pipe" with "smaller pipes beside it" extended across the ceiling. While there was an icebox, where a stove should have been someone had painted "a pastoral scene of trees and birds," and there was neither a toilet nor running water.

In the small space, Lucy's mother and Lucy's four-year-old sister Sylvia shared a bed. Westmoreland arrived just in time to witness Sylvia wetting the bed. Lucy's brother, nine-year-old William, slept on a fold-out cot. The backdoor looked out into a yard, across which "empty cans and paper" were strewn, and when the wind blew it brought through the small room the smell of urine and garbage. Neither Lucy nor her mother, Hattie Savage, were especially forthcoming nor in very good moods during the interview. They had hoped that Westmoreland was there to help Lucy find a job. Alas, she was not.[77]

Many young black poor and working-class people interviewed expertly understood Jim Crowed DC's multiple geographies and most saw themselves as leaving eventually. Until then they used the spaces they could, some of which were sanctioned, others just in reach. Three public spaces stand out in Southwest DC's geography. Willow Tree Playground was at the northern tip of Southwest, right on the border where Southwest met the encroaching National Mall. The Southwest Settlement or

Community House was centrally located and offered programming and services for both young people and adults in Southwest. And the Columbus Fountain was a public space but had not been created as a public park. Still, many young people, black and white, used it as such.

Despite the Hoover Field staff person's insistence that African American young people had ample spaces to play in Southwest, Southwest actually had only one black municipal playground. Willow Tree Playground had replaced Willow Tree Alley in 1913, by order of the Alley Dwelling Authority (and by 1940, it would be replaced by federal buildings). Located in the northeastern section of Southwest, just below the National Mall and what would become the south side of museum row, Willow Tree Playground was on almost two acres of land, surrounded by a fence, and had cost the federal government $25,000 for its construction and its equipment. In 1925, when it was researched by Howard sociology professor William Henry Jones, it included a "shelter house," a fountain, a piano, five benches, three "baby swings," eight regular swings, eight seesaws, two slides, one "sandpile" (sandbox), a small wading pool, two "kindergarten tables," one "kindergarten bench," one set of parallel bars, one balance bar, two "tether[ball] poles," a baseball area, a basketball court, and a tennis court. In 1924, the playground recorded over 16,000 young people participating in various activities including baseball, basketball, soccer, tennis, "schlag" ball (a game like baseball but which was played with a volleyball and without a bat), storytelling, and kindergarten programming. It was staffed by a groundskeeper and a director.[78]

By the hot July afternoon in 1938 when Thomas Davis surveyed it for Frazier's project, the playground had added a dodgeball court, a place to play horseshoes, and a "small grove of willow trees." Willow Tree Playground served a "free lunch around noon" and on many days it saw as many as 400 young people, according to the director, Mrs. Robinson. Robinson described the surrounding community of Southwest as not only a "red light district," but also a section where "folks don't believe in marriage," and where "some children don't even know who their parents are." Robinson had been supervising the playground for nearly twelve years and she described her long hours and the multiple projects for which she was responsible. A large "pile of trash, some of which had been burned," sat in the middle of the playground as Robinson lamented that she got little help from her assistants and only a mere "$1560 a year," equivalent to approximately a $25,000 contemporary annual salary. It was "no easy job," she said, supervising all the children, mediating disputes, of which she said there were plenty because "these boys and girls don't know anything but cutting with knives and throwing rocks; they want to fight all the time," and "they will steal anything they can get their hands on." Despite Robinson's description, on that day in July Davis found some kids were having "an impromptu track meet," a group of girls sat in a corner "making raffia baskets," "small kids play[ed] in a large sand box," and two games of chess—one between "two old men" and one between "two little boys"—took place at some lunch tables. When one boy threatened to throw a rock at another child, Mrs. Robinson interrupted her interview to intervene. Then she stepped into the "field house for a minute or two [to] get a little rest." Soon Davis noticed a "white policeman came on the grounds and walk[ed] slowly around near the field house." His presence did not go unnoticed by most of the children. It caused a "silence" to come over the playground, specifically among "many of the kids who had been quite noisy." But "several groups of [adolescent] boys, paid no attention to him when he approached" them. Instead, they continued what they had been doing.

There were rumors, according to Mrs. Robinson, "that they [were] going to close this playground and put some government building down here." Robinson hoped it was not the case, saying, "These kids really need this place. They do not have any place to play." Despite Mrs. Robinson's general negative opinion about the inherent natures of the kids from Southwest, and their parents, she expressed the importance of a recreational place for them. Willow Tree Playground was of significant importance in Southwest as the only black playground that was open year-round. The other youth recreational spaces were those connected with schools, like the A. J. Bowen schoolyard and the Randall Junior

High School recreation center, only open during school hours. Robinson thought that the park was "a lovely place. The prettiest we have" in Southwest.[79]

By 1940, the block Willow Tree Playground sat on would house the new Social Security Building, a building whose programs and benefits African Americans had had little access to generally during the Depression.[80] For young people who frequented Willow Tree it was not only some place they were fed, it was a free and open space, a space of beauty, and a place where they got an opportunity to engage with their peers socially, and in play felt free enough to take up space with both their bodies and their voices. Still, it was also a place where children did not forget and continued to learn about their racial and positional identities, both through the surveillance and stern supervision of Mrs. Robinson and her staff and that of the more powerful state. Just five days before Frazier's interviewer made his visit to Willow Tree Playground, an interracial group of community activists had staged a protest against police brutality. Some 2,000 people, mostly African American, and many children and young people carrying placards inscribed with "You May be Next," "Stop Police Murders," and comparing DC to Scottsboro, marched through Northwest, while "10,000 sympathizers watch[ed] from the sidelines."[81] The children's fearful and vigilant response to the police officer's walk-through of Willow Tree Playground, as well as the conscious nonchalant defiance of the teenage boys, evidenced the clear and multiple understandings of and the negotiations young people had with both whiteness and state-sponsored violence even in a space they partly felt, at least, was theirs.

Frazier noted that public spaces like Willow Tree Park were not frequented by middle- and upper-class black Washingtonians, who preferred "conspicuous consumption," travel, club and college fraternity activities, the Elks Lodge, and, through the privileges of mobility and income, access to places like the amusement park Suburban Gardens, Highland Beach, and Carr's Beach in Maryland.[82] For most poor and working-class DC folks, however, young people like Esther Wright, a fourteen-year-old Southwest resident and Randall Junior High School student, whose father, Robert, was a "laborer," and whose mother, Lula, was a domestic, the black amusement park Suburban Gardens in Deanwood, Northeast DC, or the E. Madison Hall Excursion Boat, for example, were financially inaccessible. On the day before July Fourth in 1938, when Esther sat with interviewer Laura Lee at the lavish and lush "Speedway" at Potomac Park, she wished she could afford to visit the amusement park, saying, in a hushed tone, she "dislike[d] sittin' in the house all the time."[83]

The Southwest Community Center or House was another sanctioned location that provided space and programming at low to no cost. While Southwest was described as devoid of any "community institutions," Southwest House was actually a fixture.[84] The Southwest House that young people referenced was not the first iteration of a settlement house in Southwest. W. E. B. Du Bois lauded an earlier "Colored Settlement House" that had been organized by social reformer Charles W. Weller in 1902, some seven years before the publication of Weller's *Neglected Neighbors*. The Southwest Colored Settlement House was located on First and M Streets, in an ill-equipped building without running water. Nonetheless, the settlement house provided day care, home visits, and training on thrift, housekeeping, temperance, and sewing, all tenets of the racial uplift agenda of the early twentieth century.[85] Solely volunteer supported, sometime between 1910 and 1920 the Southwest's Colored Settlement House went out of existence. In the wake of 1919's racial violence, though, "socially minded" Northwest resident Alma J. Scott organized support for a new settlement house for Southwest.[86]

By 1938 the Southwest Settlement House, with Scott at the helm, was one of the only remaining black settlement houses in Washington, DC. Located at the corner of Second and E Streets, the community institution emerged out of Scott's "zeal." Scott, who had lived through DC's 1919 riot, was spurred by the case of convicted murderer, young African American Josephine Berry, twenty-two years old and a mere seventy-eight (or ninety) pounds depending on whether the *Baltimore Afro-*

American or the *Washington Post* was reporting. Berry had allegedly killed her "rival" Ada Bush in the months after DC's Red Summer.[87]

In contrast to the reports in 1920 of Berry and her commuted sentence, which identified her victim as another young woman, intimating that they had fought over a beau, Scott, when she was interviewed in 1938, told a slightly different story, that of a young woman who had killed a young man, portraying both as "victims of circumstance," "unfortunate people [who] had been neglected by the more fortunate ones and who were left to seek their own forms of recreation."[88] Scott, and the 1932 article that interviewed her staff person Lillian Dotson, both noted that Scott had "made some investigations" into the young woman's life, "survey[ing the] living conditions in the S.W. section in order to find the causes behind the killing." Scott, "horrified" at her findings, "immediately began agitation for doing something about it." She lobbied the national Women's Christian Temperance Union in the early 1920s for funds to support the creation of the center. She convinced the WCTU and others of the relationship between the spatiality of poverty and violence. Out of this came the Southwest Settlement House, to serve a "Negro" neighborhood of "slums, alley dwellings, poor housing, vice, crime, etc."[89]

The community center began in 1921 as the "Mother-Child Center," both as a result of Scott's presence at and pressure on the WCTU, but also likely as a part of a national "professional" movement in reform, which included parent education in childrearing methods and baby wellness centers.[90] For example, just a few doors down from the House was the Mothers Health Association, which provided "scientific methods of contraception" and a segregated clinic twice a week. In their promotional materials, they cited three of Southwest's five census tracts as ones where there was a high rate of "children committed to institutions and placed on probation by the Juvenile Court," "juvenile delinquency," "deaths from tuberculosis," "infant mortality," and "stillborn babies," so clearly it was a community ripe for social services.[91]

The Southwest Settlement House initially offered mostly nursery services at its L Street and South Capitol location on the border of Southeast. But by 1932 it had expanded and had moved to its third location from Third Street between F and G Streets to Second and E Streets. In addition to its nursery school services, it also offered a daily food pantry, "distributing from 250 to 300 loaves of bread to needy families every day"; space for an array of youth club meetings including the Girl Reserves Club, the Soap Culture Club, the Boy Scouts, Dramatic Club, the Junior Art Club; and parent education training, including the "Mothers and First Aid" clubs, which hosted speakers from Howard University. Its third home in Southwest, a three-story building on the corner of Second and E Streets, "formerly the Old Trent Saloon," had "10 or 11 rooms." The first floor held "two ping pong tables, a pool table and a piano," and a "quiet" part, where girls played "jig saw puzzles and jacks, etc." While the boys mostly used the area with the pool table and the piano, the old bar "dispensed" milk for babies.

The second floor had a kitchen, "a room used for eating purposes," and another space for "club meetings and activities that necessitate[d] the use of tables and chairs (i.e. drawing, etc.)," Scott's office, and another "general reception room" that also doubled as a room for club meetings. The top floor housed the nursery school program, which included two staff bedrooms, three other rooms, and a "bath," and served about fifteen children a day from 7 a.m. until sometimes "after nine if the mother had to work overtime."[92]

While there was a service and a membership fee for participation in House activities, "no one pays," noted researcher Ruth Bittler. At the nursery school, "no child [was] turned away" if the mother could not afford the "25 cents per day per child," and the child received three meals a day. While the House was not able to afford medical staff for the nursery school, they received the services of a few "volunteer doctors." In addition, the New Deal's National Youth Administration provided some funds to supplement salaries for nursery school staff, who made home visits to meet with parents. The House also employed a full-time "girls worker" and a full-time "boys worker." Alma Scott reported that some "60,000 [children] go through the house in one year," and that "at present there were 800." (Interviewer Ruth Bittler, in her transcript, cautioned that the numbers were not to be "taken too literally," because funding from the Community Chest was "based on attendance figures," and Bittler reasoned that the numbers were probably inflated.)

During the summer the street out front of Southwest House was closed and became a volleyball court with net and all. Classes offered included boxing, "gymnastic stunts," a nature study class, arts and crafts, and a clay modeling class. There were also numerous sports activities and games, like basketball, dodgeball, Ping-Pong, checkers, baseball, and softball. Friday evenings often included a "planned party (to encourage regular attendance)" and young people received "lecture[s] on character building" by Father O'Neill of the St. Vincent DePaul Catholic Church just over South Capitol in Southeast. As a space for young people, aimed at "giv[ing] youth a chance for full development into manhood and womanhood unhampered by the lack of proper facilities" and at "safeguard[ing] youth by giving them the opportunity of wholesome recreational facilities through an adequate supply of outlets, that delinquency may always be at a minimum," the Southwest House had a full schedule of activities, clubs, classes, and talks.[93]

Young people certainly took advantage of the Southwest House. Seventeen-year-old James Richmond and his two friends Morris Carter and Kenneth Freeman, introduced earlier, spent part of their days ("after school hours, on weekends and throughout the summer months") at Southwest Community House.[94] Fourteen-year-old James Gray was a member of one of the settlement house's sponsored programs, the Southwest Junior Athletic Club. Gray, who lived a few doors down from Southwest House and whose younger sister was part of an editorial club, was an avid craftsman, with many "unglazed clay pieces" stored in the kitchen at the Center, including "an elephant, a football player in a crouched position and a baseball player, all about eight inches high [with a] depth of several inches." He had also stored his most prized piece, "a much carved jewelry box."[95]

Many of Susie Morgan's interviews took place at the Southwest Community House, a location she preferred to her cramped and stark alley abode. At the House, Susie intermittently participated in the Girl Reserves and the girls' baseball team. Two of her sisters, Dorothy, eighteen, and Catherine, thirteen, also attended activities at the Settlement House. Catherine had marched as part of the Southwest Community House section in the Youth Parade that April, where the Settlement House was represented by "girls pushing baby carriages gaily decorated in crepe paper" and a contingent of girls on roller skates, sporting their "sweaters bearing the Girl Reserves triangle" badge. Susie's interviewer, Laura Lee, commented that the Southwest Settlement House "made a good showing as only one of the two remaining houses [that] participated" in the Youth Parade.[96]

Southwest Settlement House was an important community institution. It was a meeting and organizing place for Southwest adults, and it provided a relatively safe place for young people, many of whom lived in poverty and near poverty, and in overcrowded homes too small for the family even, but which nonetheless took in lodgers to help supplement the family economy. Some young people negotiated neglect at home, while others experienced safety, security, and care there. Both often experienced the struggles of economic limitations. Either way, Southwest House was a second home, a place to spread out, to play and argue, to do homework or make (and store) art in a quiet corner, to access adults whose job it was to be attentive. Susie Morgan sometimes came to Southwest House to "help" out rather than to socialize with the other girls. Sixteen-year-old Harold Jones, for example, "went there often," even though he had "*never* belonged to any clubs at the Community Center" (emphasis added).[97] At the House, young people were fed, received hand-me-down clothes, and enjoyed exercise and leisure spaces and activities with their friends. Many young girls in particular, Susie Morgan and Esther Wright included, negotiated potentially dangerous Southwest sites and solicitous male attention to get to and from Southwest House.

Southwest Settlement House was a space that was sanctioned by middle-class reformers, as it had been founded by them. Meant to provide supervised and appropriate programming for young people, it did just that and it was popular. But like sidewalks where James Richmond and his friends "lolled," or corner lots where Myron Ross's father "play[ed] community checkers with the men of the neighborhood," Southwest House was at least partly popular because it was a free recreational and social place.[98] As Ruth Bittler and Alma Scott noted, the Southwest House had a nominal fee, but few paid it.

The Columbus Fountain was also a free, public, but not necessarily sanctioned, space. The Columbus Fountain outside Union Station served as a convenient, working-class and interracial, and thus not entirely "respectable," place of recreation for many of DC's young people.[99] Lobbied for by the local Knights of Columbus, funded and built by congressional mandate, and dedicated in 1912, the fountain stood at the front of Union Station along the semicircle of Massachusetts Avenue where Louisiana and Delaware Avenues intersected, directly facing the Capitol grounds of the National Mall. Co-created by Daniel Burnham, a renowned architect and member of the 1901 City Beautiful committee who had designed Union Station, the fountain was a monument to Columbus's "discovery of the western hemisphere." A statue of Columbus stood flanked on one side by a remembrance of "the old world" in the form of a white "patriarchal elder," and on the other side by "the new world," represented by a crouched indigenous young man. A large recumbent lion stood guard and a young maiden represented the "spirit of discovery."[100] The racist imagery of the sculpture was a visual manifestation and reminder of the juxtapositions of DC's national and world symbolism and its reality of oppressive and restrictive policies and practices for different groups of people over time.

Many young people referenced the fountain as part of their leisure habits—going "up to the Fountain to walk around." Hanging out at the fountain did not involve spending money, because, as Susie Morgan discovered, the ten-cent price of vanilla wafers at the station was too expensive for most of the young people. The fountain's space also allowed for covert sexual activity, as it was conveniently surrounded by obscuring bushes. James Gray, fourteen, who stored his sculptures at the Southwest House, called the fountain a "playhouse." James rather scornfully discussed the activities of some of his male peers at the fountain: "stay[ing] up there till late hours at night"; "tak[ing] girls up [there.]" The police, he said, had "got wise and [rode] around the grounds in police cars[, shining] their torches through all the bushes and pick[ing] up [anyone] they saw."[101]

The no-charge, proximal, and relatively unsupervised and mostly undersurveilled space of the fountain made it appealing. Seventeen-year-old Southwest resident Ellsworth Davis, "a good Christian" and a Boy Scout, commented that sexual activity was an affordable recreational pastime. "What else is there?" Ellsworth wondered. "A fellow," he said, "can run with a bunch of girls without money, but everything else costs like hell." Fifteen-year-old Nathaniel Smith of Sullivan's Court commented that prices for picture shows ran from ten to twenty cents depending on the day of the week and time of day, and still were prohibitive.[102]

Premarital, likely unprotected, and sometimes interracial sex was not the only thing happening at the fountain. Susie Morgan recounted a fight she and her crew had with a group of white boys there on the Tuesday night in June 1938 when Joe Louis fought his rematch with Max Schmeling. She had not listened to the fight because she "was up at the fountain." Susie's altercation started because "white boys kept going by and saying Schmeling was going to win." She had ignored them at first, but eventually, as the boys kept provoking, "we started fighting," she said. When the police arrived, the boys ran, but Susie said proudly, "I did not!" This moment of Louis's important win, or in Susie's case his potential loss, bore the weight of race pride (and would come to symbolize the triumph of democracy over an emerging totalitarian Germany.) Here Susie insisted on her bravery, in this case in the face of both white boys and the police, crafting her narrative around her fierce courage to stand her ground.[103]

Twenty-one-year-old Joseph Knight and his "gang" moved throughout the city freely, despite police surveillance. They "roam[ed]" about Southwest, "making nuisances of ourselves," eating, drinking and dancing with white girls in Southeast, and having fistfights at the Columbus Fountain outside Union Station.[104] While the fountain was an interracial space—pictorial evidence showed young white and black boys having an "outdoor lunch," eating watermelon together in the sunshine, their clothes wet from the fountain's waters—under the cover of night the fountain was a more complicated interracial place, as evidenced by Susie's narrative.[105] Joseph Knight declared, "White fellows objected to us coming up there," and "each time we met there was a fight." He boasted that he and his bunch "usually had the best of it till the police butted in," at which point they would be "chased back down Southwest." The police had even shot at them and this had really frightened Joseph. For Joseph, fighting was "great fun," even more so when he fought white boys, echoing Myron Ross's earlier comments. However, when boys started showing up with not just their fists but "armed with knives, clubs, and guns," Joseph and his friends "decided to quit before somebody got killed," either by the police or by the other boys.

When Joseph discussed interracial social and sexual contact he attributed it to geography and class, saying that "in Southeast where there are a lot of white whores and white frowsy women, [black and white] do everything together, and it isn't limited to eating, drinking, or dancing." "Up town," Joseph continued, "where you strike the better class of white people and Negroes, they don't mix much." While black and white people might eat together in Northwest, they did not "drink or dance together." "They used to have mixed games (baseball, horseshoes, soccer, and even tennis)," Joseph remembered, "but for some reason they've stopped all that." Joseph questioned why even local prize fighting had been recently Jim Crowed in Washington, saying that "Negroes and whites play games together in other places and get along swell."[106]

For poor and working-class black young people, social reformers and black community leaders alike advocated for increased and integrated leisure and recreation spaces and activities, believing that engagement in sanctioned pastimes necessarily decreased the likelihood of what was thought of as juvenile delinquency among young black people. For example, John T. Rhines, longtime Southwest resident, local funeral director, and Southwest Civic Association leader, had advocated for a police athletic boys club in Southwest and had been denied. In his 1938 community interview, Rhines expressed his anger toward Police Commissioner Major Ernest Brown, who was already facing criticism for antiblack police brutality in the capital, saying that Brown had instead approved a club for white boys and promised "they would make [Southwest] the next one." As a result of the white boys club, Rhines stated that "juvenile delinquency for the whites [had] steadily decreased while that [of] the Negro boys [had] steadily increased." Black poor and working-class boys, without access to "a small job and some place to play," Rhines thought, could not really be "blame[d] too much." Southwest people "live[d] within their means and not over them," and deserved "some real work done" in the community.[107]

Nearly a decade after Frazier had completed his study, the National Committee on Segregation in the Nation's Capital published its report in 1948. Frazier and other prominent Howard University affiliated folks were members of the committee, as was Walter Reuther of the United Auto Workers and former First Lady Eleanor Roosevelt.[108] Funded by the Julius Rosenwald Fund, the report outlined many of the incongruities addressed and contested by Susie Morgan and Myron Ross Jr. above: Washington's symbolism as "the city of a nation," as "Democracy's great stage" upon which tourists and dignitaries alike from across the world came to see "Democracy in Action," but where researchers and policy analysts found instead "that Washington [was] not a good salesman for democracy."[109] In addition to discriminatory practices against an "African foreign minister," "a Puerto Rican Senator," "a Panama [sic] visitor," and a "Hindu woman," there were no accommodations in the downtown area; restaurants were willing only to serve a black (or black-appearing) person who stood at the counter; there was no taxi service;

theaters would not admit African Americans; and "department store clerks turn[ed] their backs at the approach of a Negro."[110] The report even cited a dog cemetery that had "erected a color bar against the burial of dogs belonging to colored people."[111]

In housing, the National Committee referred to poor black communities in DC with a term that had recently come more fully into parlance, as "ghettoes," identifying "mass segregation [as] a relatively new phenomenon in the Nation's Capital." This segregation, they said, was based on the "*myth* of a Negro invasion" (emphasis added), here referring to black migration to the city.[112] While there had been spikes in black migration, the report found that the population of African Americans had remained at about one-third of the total population overall. In contrast, it attributed segregationist policies not to a rise in black population, but to the building of new federal, public, and private real estate (e.g., "recent additions to George Washington University—forbidden to Negroes"). "Areas," the report stated, "formerly occupied by Negroes have been condemned for government buildings, parks, schools." Mostly poor and working-class African Americans were "dislodged" and "crammed tighter and tighter into the already bursting Negro ghettoes." White associations of homeowners, initially organized as "neighborhood improvement societies, interested in such things as trees and flowers, schools and parks," had "become actively concerned [with] the containment of Negroes." As a result, pockets and enclosures of poor and working-class "slums" had formed into "black belts" that appeared to "besiege the Capital."[113] Reminiscent of Charles Weller's earlier study of "alleys, tenements, and shanties in the shadow of the Nation's Capital," the report included a centerfold of photographs of overgrown backyards with broken fences, trash and half naked black children playing "in the shadow of the capital" or "near [the] Senate Office Building."[114] The National Committee's examination of "Segregation in Washington" called out DC's racial geography.

Washington, DC, had multiple geographies, of race, of class, and of gender, and for poor and working-class African American young people these geographies intersected with age. The youngest black person understood expertly the complicated nature of DC's racial discrimination and its economic adherents. Racial hostility, as a result of being in certain spaces, could not be avoided. The quotidian experiences of the young people interviewed and the accompanying ethnographic reports of the Southwest community show that the conditions of poverty and economic disparity were themselves geographic, which made "avoiding" racial hostility extremely difficult, for the condition of poverty *was* one of racial hostility.

For African American young people, limited by the depressed economy and the racial segregation of the District, the claiming and reappropriating of public spaces into places of recreation, leisure, and community was an important part of their relationship with both the experienced and imagined landscapes of the capital city. Susie Morgan and Joseph Knight's stories of their fights with white kids at the fountain and Susie's courage in the face of the police, with whom she interacted quite often, illustrate their sense of entitlement to spaces not meant for them. That did not mean, however, that they did not participate in sanctioned recreation and leisure activities and use designated spaces. For example, thirteen-year-old Quenton Porter's mother, Viola, found Northwest apartment living so "confining and depressive to children," she let both Quenton and his brother "use the Y *and* the gang as outlcts" (emphasis added), in spite of knowing that likely her boys were not "behaving" all the time.[115]

Young people like Susie Morgan and Myron Ross Jr., through their speech and action, called for freedom of mobility, safety from racial violence and trauma, and spaces, both public and private, of their own. Susie, for example, marveled at interviewer Laura Lee's seemingly large Northwest home in comparison to her own, asking upon her first visit to Lee's home "do people live in all these rooms here?" and asking if she could "come up and spend the summer." Like Myron Ross Jr., Susie also lamented that she had no place to study at home, sharing her living space with so many people. In one of the last documents from Susie, she tells Laura Lee in a letter, "I would like to have a room all to myself with a desk in it and anything I need."[116]

Out of this perspicuity, Susie Morgan appropriated the Lincoln Memorial Reflecting Pool. But Susie's occupation was in line with other black protests at this important national shrine. In 1926, four years after the monument's dedication, an audience of two thousand mostly African Americans gathered for a mass religious service. And a year after Susie's action, Marian Anderson performed an Easter Sunday concert on the steps directly in front of Lincoln at the Lincoln Memorial. DC's Daughters of the American Revolution had denied Anderson access to Constitution Hall and the DC Board of Education had also refused to allow her to perform in white Central High School's auditorium. Susie may well have been in the crowd of 75,000 people on that April day in 1939. In 1941, labor leader A. Philip Randolph had only to threaten a march and demonstration at the Lincoln Memorial to encourage President Franklin D. Roosevelt to issue Executive Order 8802 banning racial discrimination in defense industry jobs. And in 1943, Randolph led an interracial, interfaith "prayer pilgrimage" to the monument to celebrate Lincoln's birthday.[117]

Susie and Myron's contestations over space were not anomalies in the capital. In the spring of 1938, the run of George Gershwin's *Porgy and Bess* at DC's "whites-only" National Theater featured black actors and singers, some of whom were affiliated with Howard University's music department. At first the National had refused to allow black patrons at the performance, but the theater soon changed its policy, albeit briefly, after uproar from the local community and after the performers vowed not to appear for a segregated audience.[118]

Still, Southwest, and other poor and working-class black neighborhoods in Washington, DC, had more pressing problems. It appeared unsafe and unsanitary, "dilapidated and shabby," to social researchers and reformers, and had for much of the early twentieth century.[119] These communities faced the constant threat of redevelopment; Southwest in particular experienced continual encroachment of the federal core, and all were the perpetual laboratories for social scientific examination and reform that saw their predominant blackness and poverty as ripe for both structural *and* cultural rehabilitation.

What comes through in the narratives above is that black poor and working-class young people navigated and negotiated the complex terrain of Jim Crow DC. Young people's mobility, sometimes into spaces out of which they were ultimately chased by white youth, by the police, and by black adults, through spaces in which they were harassed or harmed, highlights the possibilities and desirability of, and risks taken for, movement by young black bodies in the small racialized, socially stratified, and gendered geographies of Washington, DC. Asserting their authorial subjective selves, black poor and working-class young people ventured outside of their assigned places, reappropriated sidewalks, doorways, playgrounds, and even national monuments. For both young people and adults, their physical presence in public spaces that had not been intended for black young or black poor, and sometimes just black, bodies demonstrated the ways in which they claimed a national identity, especially significant in the racially segregated US capital. As young Susie Morgan stated about swimming in the Lincoln Memorial Reflecting Pool, "Course we know we ain't got no business there, but that's why we go in."[120]

Figure 3.1. "Washington, D.C. Science class in a Negro high school." Marjorie Collins, photographer, Farm Security Administration, March 1942. Library of Congress, Prints & Photographs Division, FSA/OWI Collection [LC-DIG-fsa-8d20292].

3

"I Would Carry a Sign"

The Politics of Black Adolescent Personality Development

The Jim Crow world was a shrunken thing, not simply because of its restrictions and where one could or couldn't go,
but by its limits on what one could think, imagine, dream,
be—the actual diminution of one's ability to realize the full
possibilities of one's humanity.
—Thomas Holt, "'A Story of Ordinary Human Beings': The
Sources of Du Bois's Historical Imagination"[1]

I think a Negro could do any job as well if not better than
any white man. . . . somewhere in this country there is a Negro who could even handle the job of President, and do a
good job of it.
—Myron Ross Jr., Southwest DC, 1938

Myron Ross Jr.'s first interview with Dennis Nelson happened as they
sat "on the running board of a car parked just in front of the Anthony
Bowen School Playground." Myron had been "playing ball" in the playground located at the back of the school in the square block bordered
by First, M, Delaware, and L Streets and surrounded by trees in Southwest.[2] Nelson described Myron as "dress[ed] neatly but not well." Myron
was "a tall, lithe, well-built, dark brown Negro boy," the eldest of Laura
Evelyn Ross and Myron Ross Sr.'s nine children. As seen earlier, Myron
had lived in Southwest for his entire life. The Rosses, despite Frazier's
categorization of them as decidedly middle class due to Myron Ross
Sr.'s city employment with the District Fire Department, were not at all

financially secure. Their home was described as a "dilapidated six-room house, surrounded by [the] still more dilapidated and ill-kept structures [of Southwest.]" Nelson said the home was "neglected, poorly furnished, [with] wall paper, floors and windows [all] in much need of repair." Interviews were often conducted "thirty or forty yards from the house" because Nelson found Myron's full house "disheveled," too "noisy and playful."[3]

Myron was a rising sophomore at Armstrong High School the summer he was interviewed. He belonged to the Boy Scouts, where his father was "Chairman" of his "troop committee" and he was "Patrol Leader and Assistant Scoutmaster." He also belonged to the coed Baron's Social Club, to which he paid ten cents in dues each week and served as vice president; the history club at school because he was "very interested in history"; and the track team. In addition to his siblings, his large household included random stray and "bedraggled pets," "elaborate [tropical fish] aquariums equipped with electrical devices for heating and lighting," and his father's extensive ham radio operating equipment. He was "a good student" with "unusual aesthetic tastes," "a real boy," "a fair athlete," and "possess[ed] a very intelligent face and [a] pleasing personality." To Nelson, Myron seemed "deliberate in his thinking and in whatever he ha[d] to say"; he "seldom smile[d when] he talk[ed], and usually converse[d] in such a manner as to leave the impression that he [sought] information rather than proffer[ed] it."[4]

Frazier assessed many of the poor and working-class young people interviewed for the project as "sullen," as generally politically disengaged, and "accommodated to their inferior status."[5] He believed that they had sublimated their anger and resentment about the conditions under which they lived, acting out only in criminal behavior, and that they did not "seek to reconstruct their world by social action."[6] Of course, this depends on how one defines social action. Susie Morgan and her friends, as we saw in the last chapter, reappropriated the Lincoln Memorial Reflecting Pool as their swimming hole. Their interplay with both Lincoln and the police at a potentially dangerous moment in the midst of a wave of police brutality and an anti-police-brutality campaign in Washington, DC, was certainly both an attempt at social action and to reconstruct their world.

And Myron Ross had not "deeply suppressed" his rage—about his experiences as a Boy Scout, at the institutions that denied his father promotion, nor at the white boys who played in his neighborhood in a park he was not allowed to enter. And Myron Ross was not the only young person, as Frazier's collaborator psychiatrist Harry Stack Sullivan noted, who "took himself, his past, and the problematic future with considerable and rather realistic seriousness."[7] As you will see in this chapter, many of the young people interviewed were not only aware of the politics of race and space in the capital city, they worked to make meaning of it and had opinions about the ways those politics and the conditions they created touched their lives and the lives of those with whom they shared communities.

Initially, Myron was skeptical of Sullivan's interest in him. "Suspicious," in Myron's words, as he usually was when "white people get all solicitous." He had felt "funny and uncomfortable" at first when Sullivan "asked questions about racial matters," and Myron was not sure whether that had been because Sullivan was "a white man and [Myron] a Negro or just that the subjects were touchy ones anyway." "In fact," Myron noted, Sullivan had been "so kind and friendly-like [that Myron] had thought he was a Negro." He had asked Dennis Nelson about Sullivan's racial identity and Nelson had put in a good word for Sullivan, despite Sullivan's whiteness. Myron said he had "learned to like and trust" Sullivan eventually.[8]

For Myron, his "big family [was] a holdback to [him]." It made many things difficult: trips, clothes, toys. He remembered "hat[ing] the arrival of" a new baby, saying, "it got so it didn't look like they'd ever stop coming [. . .]. I don't think the stork stopped by here—he just stayed." And at the time of this interview, Myron feared his parents were not finished having children. While he admired his father and thought him to be "an intelligent man," from whom Myron had learned much, he "[didn't] think he['d] been so smart" in the family planning department. He noted that white families with more resources than his family had fewer children. By Myron's second interview, he was adamant that he did not "want any children," exclaiming "Heaven forbid!" and saying that he thought both his parents were "crazy." Because of his family's size, Myron lamented his lack of privacy; he shared a room with his four brothers and had an "iron locker where he [kept his] few treasures and prize belongings." With such a full house he longed for "some place [he] could call [his] own."[9]

Despite Myron's complaints about the many sacrifices he had made because of his large family, including his lack of a private space, there were some things he had come to enjoy. For example, Myron appreciated that family meals were like "picnics," especially if they had company over. They "got all the tables together through the dining room and the front room." When there were guests, aunts, and cousins, there would be "20 or 21 of us eating at the same time." Somehow, Myron marveled, even when they couldn't have new shoes or clothes, they always had enough food to eat. Myron: "My folks don't believe in stinting on food. We feed well even if at times we don't look so presentable."[10]

As the eldest, Myron was an integral part of making sure that the family functioned. "We try to work out a regular schedule among us to help with the young kids and the housework," Myron said. At his father's insistence, he and the other older children did all they could "to help mother." And while Myron did not think he was much good at "housecleaning"—he hated it—the perk was that he got "breaks," coming and going as he desired. Mostly, Myron tried to stay out of the house. The cramped quarters at least partially led to Myron's many adventures around the city: seining for minnows in Maryland, and his Boy Scout activities.[11]

It was in Myron's discussions of his travels both within and outside of DC that we get to hear his experiences with and ruminations on racial segregation. This is where he discussed his desire to find an outlet for his anger at the white-only Hoover Field playground adjacent to his home in predominantly black Southwest. A quarter of a block away from his house, the playground was, to Myron, a "large city block gone to waste." It was here, in and over this contested space, that Myron "tried [his] best to get one of the white boys mad enough to fight about it." Fighting did not make much sense to Myron for a number of reasons: because his parents did not approve, although they did see the necessity of protecting oneself; because "boys [his] size" did not fight with fists only, but rather "knives and the like"; and because Myron wanted to avoid arrest, which "would never do." Still, he was "itch[ing] to take a crack at a white guy just to see if he can take it like he can dish it: stand as man to man." He would "scrap if [he] could get [a white boy] to meddle with him or with anyone else in [his] presence."[12] He felt that it was unlikely that he would get this opportunity, saying "white people aren't going to mess with you unless they feel they definitely have the upper hand." But, Myron lamented, "they like to hurt your feelings and all and call you names." So, despite Myron's mother's general disapproval of fighting, for Myron fights had a place in race relations: the assertion of one's dominance, and it could be retributive. Myron thought that certainly if he ever got the chance to face a white boy in a fight that he could "easily whip" him. And we know from Myron's mother's interview that Myron Ross Sr. was training the boys to box, so Myron Jr. may have well been correct about his ability to come out on top.[13]

As discussed in the previous section, Myron was clear about the spatiality of Jim Crow in DC, which Myron thought was "crazy": that department stores, theaters, and restaurants refused to accommodate black patrons; that though there were segregated churches, whites often came to Myron's church and "seem[ed] to enjoy themselves"; that there were separate swimming facilities and no places to swim in Southwest. But Myron had further observations. He noted that white people were unwilling to address African Americans respectfully by using "Mr., Mrs., or Miss," unless, he said, there was an ulterior motive that usually involved an exchange of money. As he and Nelson sat talking outside of his home, Myron "pointed to a white peddler across the street, canvassing from house to house." "Take that guy across the street," Myron said. "He'd call you Sweetheart to sell his stuff. Everybody is Mr. and Mrs., but just wait until he gets on his feet or through with the sale, he's ready to call you Joe, Sam, or Mary."[14]

Deference, Myron thought, was a useful tactic especially if "you [had] some white person you want[ed] to cultivate and expect[ed] to get something out of." Myron had learned from his parents that "people will do a whole lot more for you [when you] act as gentlemanly as possible." He had watched his father doing odd jobs for white people and had seen the way he "got along swell and everybody liked him." Myron had taken the same approach with his paper delivery route in Southeast where most of his customers had been white. He told Nelson he had yes Ma'am-ed or no Ma'am-ed as necessary in order "to shittle [i.e., squeeze] something out [of them.]" He thought "they liked it, but [he had] hated it every time [he] did it." Still, it had worked: "they learned to trust [him.]" He even began to do some dog walking for some families, and at Christmas he often got monetary gifts.

This discussion led to Myron's expressions of anger, that few black people did more than merely and quietly resent being called by their first names (or any first name) by "people of that class," meaning poor white people. Rather, Myron believed that if more black people responded by calling that person also by his or her first name, "that would stop some of it."[15] Frazier assessed these lessons Myron had learned from his parents as "techniques for 'getting by,'" a remnant of Myron's mother's country roots brought inappropriately forward into the modern urban city.[16] But Myron identified politeness, respect, and deference more as methods for getting access to things, a kind of cultural capital and code-switching. And it was not merely the behavior of poor African Americans with rural origins, but anyone, including white people, who deployed these strategically.

To Myron, Jim Crow also meant that black people did not "get as good chances for jobs as white people." In most cases, he said, "jobs prefer a white face to experience," which gave white men the ability to "choose" what they wanted. This was not only unfair, in Myron's estimation, but it resulted in an inaccurate assessment of the capabilities of African Americans. "I think a Negro could do any job as well if not better than any white man," Myron stated, adding, "somewhere in this country there is a Negro who could even handle the job of President, and do a good job of it," forecasting a twenty-first century future.[17]

Myron's lived experiences thus far also made it clear that racial segregation and discrimination had an economic impact. Myron's father, Myron Ross Sr., was a prime example of this. Myron Jr. explained that his father had been "in the only Negro Fire Department for fifteen years. He [was] eligible for promotion but where would they put him?" The problem was that the captain of the firehouse had been there for thirty-five years and there were no other black firehouses to which his father could be promoted, unlike white men in firehouses who could be moved around as they became eligible for advancement. "Color again! You can't beat it!" Myron exclaimed.[18]

Influenced by the prevalence of racially discriminatory policies and their impact, Myron supported the idea of passing. One's racial identity was in fact a disadvantage if one was black. Myron had "learned" he was black in school, and despite his "satisfaction" knowing his race would not change, if he could be reborn, he sometimes wished "to be white." "Having a white face," Myron said, "would make all the difference . . . in success and failure." He admitted, "I would [pass] if I could and wouldn't think anything about it either." For this reason, Myron was especially intrigued by Booker T. Washington, who had "accomplished [much] in *spite* of color," enough that "even white people [had] to respect and admire him and the work he's done."[19]

Myron's narrative, including his experiences navigating the racially restricted city in the previous chapter, demonstrates the many layers to both his short life so far and his thinking. Myron had adapted in all the necessary ways, not just to his hyperlocal familial situation but also to the realities of his neighborhood and to the inequalities rampant in his education, saying "we study white people and white people's history, and with all that knowledge, we don't get whiter and they sure don't treat us like we were becoming whiter."[20] Like many of his peers, Myron identified himself as a sexual person, and had opinions on the importance of sex education. In response to a question about his sexual history, Myron described his first sexual experience, the result of which had been a sexually transmitted infection, pubic lice, or "crabs." "Ashamed, scared, [and] miserable," Myron went to his father, but only after he had "stolen [his] mother's book of home remedies" and had been unsuccessful in treating himself. His father was surprisingly, to Myron, very understanding, but Myron wished he had gotten more information about sex either from school or his parents before he had had intercourse, saying, "I think a father or a teacher should give you first-hand information from time to time without being asked."

Myron said he had gotten much of his "knowledge of sex from corners and bunches of boys," but not much of it had been helpful. There had been "a series of talks arranged on sex and health" at his school. But girls and boys were segregated and although Myron and a female friend had agreed to "exchange the information [they] got in the lectures," his friend "refused" to share what she had learned when it was over. Myron insisted that it was not out of mere "curiosity," rather he "really wanted the information." He did not think there was any "shame in the human body[:] sex, birth, babies, are all natural things and happen among birds, beasts, and man alike." He believed nothing was gained when "men [knew] men's bodies and care of them alone, and girls [only knew] women's bodies and the care of them." Myron, like many of the young people interviewed, felt strongly that he would have benefited from sexual health education that provided information about not only his own changing body but about women's bodies as well. And that while his father had been incredibly helpful in getting him treatment, not judgmental and generally approachable, Myron thought his father "ought to realize [that his children would] like to know about such things before [they] run across such experiences."[21]

Myron and his peers shared an understanding of themselves as relational people, but many of the young women interviewed offered considerably less information about their burgeoning sexual identities. Young women were more reticent to divulge whether or not they were sexually active without some coaxing and encouragement from the interviewer that they would not be judged. Young women like Lucy Savage (seventeen), Esther Wright (fourteen), or Rosella Hillman (thirteen) either had boyfriends, had had a boyfriend but didn't want one currently, or were lovelorn, but they all shared little about their sexual experiences. Even when they were not interested in marriage, it did not mean they were not interested in sex (more on this in the next chapter.) Many young people's parents, mothers in particular, discussed the importance of educating their children about sex and reproduction, especially girls. Some parents often assumed that boys would get the information on the streets, while others told sons engaged in sports programs that sexual activity would decrease their athletic abilities. Young people corroborated in their interviews, as Myron did, that this information was indeed crucial, expressing dissatisfaction with access to sex education at school and sometimes at home, and saying that most of the information they had gotten from friends or older siblings was not very accurate. Most of the girls interviewed had considerably more sexual health knowledge that they had learned directly from their mothers who, in contrast to their own upbringings, which had been frustratingly silent on menstruation and pregnancy, had intentionally included open conversations about sex with their daughters, much to Frazier's disapproval.

Relationships—familial, community, and romantic—were important to the young people interviewed. William Wright was Lula Wright's nineteen-year-old son and Esther Wright's older brother. He had apparently saved at least one of his sisters on at least one occasion from being sexually assaulted by one of his friends. Identified in Frazier's archives as a high school graduate, the 1940 census documented that he and his sisters all had only finished the ninth grade. William, like Myron, lived in Southwest with his mother, his father John Robert, a laborer, and his three sisters, on a block now home to federal buildings. There were only three large index cards left of William's interview and they answered an unrecorded question. In other interviews, William was identified as one of the leaders of a "bunch" with which several interviewees ran. None of what remains of William's interview references William's "gang," however. Rather, what remains is an explanation of how William became "Rosa's" unwitting boyfriend, then father of a child with her, and eventually her husband.[22]

William's fragmented narrative shows William's negotiation of and disappointment in adult relationships. William proudly recounted the respectful overture to and *gentlemen's agreement* he made with Rosa's boyfriend. After meeting Rosa, William approached Rosa's boyfriend, whom he described as "a nice boy," and expressed both interest in her and a desire to pursue her. Although he did not want to necessarily "bust them up," he warned her boyfriend that he was "going to make a play for her." According to William, Rosa's boyfriend "was nice about it," saying William could try and that if he "could get her it would prove that [William] was [the] better man." One night, William got his chance, although it was not quite the way he had thought it would go. They had all attended "a hop," "not a dance," insisted William, "but one of those famous rug-cutting contests." William kept his eye on Rosa and her boyfriend all night from a corner of the room. He spied his chance when he saw them arguing, Rosa looking as if "she was going to break up the party." William took the opportunity to "step in," took Rosa's hand and led her to the door. But her boyfriend intervened and "snatched her by the other hand and dragged her back into the room." William let Rosa go and returned to his corner with one hope in mind, that there would be a police raid at that moment. And lo and behold, some ten minutes later, there was. Rosa's boyfriend was long gone and

William was not far behind him, both in an effort to escape the raid. But when William noticed that Rosa had been pushed back against a table where a lamp was broken, he went back to get her, which put him in harm's way. A policeman caught him and "hit [him] a hefty blow on the side of the head with his fist," knocking William's hat off. He and Rosa somehow got away. Later at William's house, high on adrenaline from fear and excitement, they both "felt reckless." That was the beginning of their relationship.

The next night at William's house, as they were "necking," Rosa's boyfriend showed up, calling out to William, but William got rid of him. It is unclear whether or not Rosa broke up with her boyfriend. Nevertheless, Rosa and William began to see each other. After Rosa learned she was pregnant neither she nor William saw "hair nor hide" of her boyfriend. About the boyfriend's desertion, William commented, "I can't blame him [. . .]. I only wish I had been able to steer clear too." William's thoughts about this particular situation in his life were cut short, for Rosa approached him and interviewer Dennis Nelson as they talked on the corner. In the 1940 census, William's registered occupation mirrored that of his father's: "laborer," and a "Rose Mary" is listed as residing with the Wrights and as William's wife, but there does not appear to be a child in the household the appropriate age to be the baby with which Rosa was supposed to have been pregnant at the time of the interview.[23]

In this fragmented narrative, a self-identified chivalrous William Wright risked his safety to rescue Rosa in a police raid. He liked her enough and had successfully "taken her" away from her boyfriend. But no sooner did he feel saddled with her, wishing he had "steer[ed] clear," escaped as her boyfriend had. Within the next two years he would be married.[24] William's boyhood was cut short by the long-term consequences of a particular kind of burgeoning and masculinist manhood that required him to *possess* Rosa. His displays of chivalry and his "gentleman's agreement" aside, Rosa starts out as an object to be "taken away" from the man who owns her, the physical tussle over her in the party evidence of this. Additionally, it is clear that not all young women were disinterested in marriage. Living in the moment, like Myron had with this first sexual experience, could and did have longer term effects than necessarily intended—crabs, marriage. And police raids of Southwest youth activities were commonplace realities, enough so that one could wish for one and have the wish come true.

The above ruminations on Jim Crow, sexuality, and relationships stand in contrast to *Negro Youth at the Crossways* findings about the young people interviewed. Frazier, and St. Clair Drake in his introduction to the 1967 edition, identified a lack of community involvement, a lack of interest in social movements, and a general apathy, attributing these all to young people's "rural background and low economic status."[25] But young people were indeed aware of the injustices of their city and engaged in both actions against and the cultivation of ideas about them. Twenty-three-year-old Anne Winston, for example, working on a Works Progress Administration project in the Agriculture Department, attended, along with her mother, the newly formed interracial Women's Trade Union League meeting, where she participated in organizing a letter writing campaign and a boycott against the laundry that had recently fired an employee for participation in union activities.[26]

Seventeen-year-old Joseph Ward was "president" of the Society Gents Club, an organization Frazier described disparagingly, and which will be discussed further in the next section.[27] Despite Joseph's participation in this bunch, he also expressed opinions about the boycott against the Peoples Drug Store in DC, as did other young people. In the summer of 1938, the New Negro Alliance's "Don't Buy Where You Can't Work" or "Jobs for Negroes" campaign was in its early months of targeting the Peoples Drug Store for its refusal to hire black clerks despite having a significant number of black patrons.[28] Joseph felt strongly that "the hearts of white men [could not] be changed, so the only solution [was] better and bigger business[es] by Negroes which will hire Negro youth." Black patronage at black businesses was the only way to deal with employment

Figure 3.2. "Washington, D.C. Two Negro boys reading the funnies on a door-step." Gordon Parks, photographer, Farm Security Administration, November 1942. Library of Congress, Prints & Photographs Division, FSA/OWI Collection [LC-DIG-fsa-8d23347].

discrimination. Joseph did not see much value in the boycott and picketing being staged in Northwest: "I don't think that's going to be of great benefit to Negroes." He was concerned that those African Americans who did hold jobs in white establishments would be fired as a result of the action and in general one or two black hires at the drugstore would not "be of great financial benefit to the race." Rather he thought that the funds being used to support the action could be spent on opening up a "first class" black drugstore, which would be "advertis[ed] widely" and patronized by African Americans in the city. He saw the picket as a distraction: black folks in the city were "letting [their] own businesses suffer while [they] tried to stifle somebody else's." He was also concerned that the action made "us look ridiculous."[29]

Joseph's comments about the New Negro Alliance–sponsored political action are evidence that not only was he aware of what was happening outside of his neighborhood (the Peoples Drug Store was in Northwest), but that he had an informed and complicated opinion. He understood that policy, whether corporate or legislative, would not change personal feelings and racist beliefs, gesturing toward a quasi-nationalist philosophy rooted in self-reliance, while also alluding to concerns about respectable comportment and their possible consequences. Moreover, he reminded the interviewer that young people faced serious unemployment. Joseph was not the only young person who commented on the early civil rights campaign and whose answers illustrate the complexity of young people's understandings of racial politics in their segregated city.

Many of the young people expressed displeasure with G. David Houston, principal of Myron Ross's Armstrong High School, who had crossed the picket line, saying he had "the God given right to deal where [he] please[d] and buy what [he] want[ed]."[30] Gloria Tinner, sixteen, criticized Houston, saying he was "supposed to be an educator and leader of his race." She thought he "should be tarred and feathered for going in there," commenting that he had "no race pride whatsoever." Gloria said she "wouldn't have the nerve to walk in there while our people are attempting to get better jobs for Negroes."[31]

Nineteen-year-old "lower class" Bernadyne Snowden was a resident of Northeast. In response to the question of whether she was "interested in the N. N. A.," Bernadyne said she had "become interested since they [were] picketing." She knew what the acronym stood for and that they were working "to get employment for Negroes." Like some of the other girls, Bernadyne insisted she would not cross the picket line; in addition, Bernadyne said she would "carry a sign." "I'd think," she said, "any young person interested in getting a job of any kind would be more than willing to carry a sign." Interviewer Isadore Miles asked Bernadyne if her "parents [were] opposed to movement[s] like NNA." Bernadyne said that her parents were supportive. They were concerned though that the organization and the protesters would "weaken before it [was] over." Bernadyne did not think so. She "[was] praying for them to hold out." Bernadyne's narrative stands in stark contrast to not only some of her contemporaries but also to St. Clair Drake's charge of apathy among poor and working-class young people.[32]

Seventeen-year-old Northwest resident Verra Couzens asked her interviewer whether the interviewer was aware that there was picketing at the Peoples Drug Store and what they thought about it. Her interviewer responded: "They seem to feel they should work there," and turned the question back to Verra. Verra was not quite certain what to think, at first saying she did not know. It had been about five months since the picketing had started and she did not think it was working: "It seems to me that if the man wanted to hire colored he would have hired colored long ago." She wondered why they should boycott white-owned Peoples Drug Store, but not "all of these [Jewish-owned] stores in colored neighborhoods," where black people shopped regularly. Still, she did not plan to cross the picket line.[33] Verra's Northwest neighbor, twelve-year-old Carolyn Taylor, was not sure "whether she approved of the picketing or not, [. . . although] she understood the purpose all right."[34] Carolyn insisted, though, that she would indeed cross the picket line, saying that "she would go into the store if there was anything in there that she wanted on sale; she would pay no attention to the signs." Her right as a consumer was to "get articles where they were cheapest." Moreover, "she had never seen colored clerks except in colored drug stores," and saw the action as being futile. She believed that "Negroes should stick to their own race—[and] try to get work in colored drug stores."[35]

The Meade sisters of Southeast were interviewed together. Both "lower class girls" were single and mothers. They were asked if they "approve[d] of the picketing." Older sister Addie, nineteen, a maid in a private home, responded by saying that she believed there should be both "as many colored working in the stores as whites" and that "there should be more colored drug stores." Her younger sister by a year, Minnie, a waitress at a National Youth Administration school, countered that "you [couldn't] blame everything on white people." She thought it was quite "natural" that white people would seek to employ other white people, since "colored people will naturally employ colored people." She agreed with her sister that there should be "more colored people in power [with] businesses [so that they could] employ colored." At which, Addie reiterated that there should be more black-owned drugstores, citing that there was "only one" in all of Southeast.[36]

Sixteen-year-old Alice Williams was in her second interview with Laura Lee when she expressed her opinions on the boycott, but not before she declared her suspicions of Lee's intentions. The African American eleventh grader had already spent one afternoon the previous week with Lee, during which she had been asked about "outstanding coloreds she admired," what she listened to on the radio, whether she ever played with white kids, and what she thought of segregation. She was curious about how questions about the "color" of God, and whether she played with dolls, "fit" into a study on "the problems of young people." Still, after voicing her uncertainties, she took advantage of Lee's listening ear.[37]

In addition to lamenting the loss of her older sister who had recently died of pneumonia and to whom she had been close, Alice discussed the death of her father, whom she missed but whose insurance money was allowing them to have a bit more economic security. She insisted that more mothers should educate their daughters on sex and sexuality as her mother had. She disapproved of spending money on boys and disparaged middle- and upper-class black parents for giving allowances to their children. Then, finally, she said she supported the NNA-sponsored boycott and picketing of the Peoples Drug Store for not hiring any black clerks. Both Alice and her friend, seventeen-year-old Frankie Meachum, expressed "approval" of the boycott, saying it was "a good idea" and long overdue. However, when they were asked if they would picket, both were aghast, responding with laughter: "No, indeed," and "Me? Walking on 14th and You [U Street]?"[38]

Joseph Ward and the other young people who discussed the NNA boycott had nuanced and variegated political understandings of their specific location and moment. Some lent support to the NNA or other actions with their physical bodies, others were willing to cross the Peoples Drug Store picket line out of necessity or cynicism about changes to racist hiring policies, or because it was their right as a capitalist consumer to get a bargain. Still others articulated ideas about alternatives to the boycott that included seeing an increase in black-owned and supported businesses. Despite what Frazier identified as "the failure of Negro youth to participate fully in the life of the community," these young people were not only aware, they took the opportunity to express strong and thoughtful opinions about political actions in Washington, DC.[39] Joseph Ward's expressions, Susie Morgan's actions, and the comments culled from Bernadyne Snowden and other African American "lower class" youth, including Myron Ross, make plain that Harry Stack Sullivan's comments about Myron, that he "took himself, his past and the problematic future with considerable and rather realistic seriousness," were true for many of the young people involved in the study.[40]

Psychiatrist Dr. Harry Stack Sullivan had taken a special interest in Myron Ross Jr. Of the twenty young people Sullivan studied, Myron "received the most attention." For Sullivan, this was not because of Myron's "eminent suitability to represent the average Negro youth. Quite the contrary, [Myron] impressed [Sullivan] as definitely unusual." While Sullivan believed that Myron likely took him to be "a probably transient phenomenon in his life, as did most of the subjects," Myron did not treat him "with amiable superficiality and inconsequence." Sullivan praised Myron's clarity in his "realization that to achieve any of the objectives that he contemplated with pleasure, he would need assistance on which he could depend." Seemingly, Sullivan saw himself as that dependable assistance, and it was Myron's awareness of this and his willingness to talk openly with Sullivan that seemed to prove Myron's uniqueness.[41]

In truth, though, many of the young people interviewed shared these characteristics. Young black poor and working-class people understood the relationship between their racial identities and their future possibilities. When they were asked about famous black individuals and what they knew of the "accomplishments of Negroes" (Carter G. Woodson, George Washington Carver, Robert Russa Moton, Frederick Douglass, Booker T. Washington, Paul Laurence Dunbar, Jack Johnson) many were quick to bring up local community folks and Joe Louis. Others lamented that they had not learned much in school about black history and thought there should be much more, including local and more recent history—like about black participation in World War I. Still others, mostly the young women, mentioned Mary McLeod Bethune and actors like Louise Beavers and Fredi Washington, even if they also criticized Peola Johnson's character in the contemporary film *Imitation of Life*. The importance of both popular culture and media representation was not lost on them.

These articulations—thoughts on local political conditions and actions, the state of sexual health and black history education, and on adult relationships, interracial, romantic, and otherwise—bring into relief the ways in which young people not only possessed desires to transform their worlds, but had already and continued to cultivate analytic frameworks about the worlds around them, frameworks that informed their engagement in their communities and how they saw and mobilized their agency in those communities.

Figure 4.1. "Street scene, Negro section, Washington, D.C." Edwin Rosskam, photographer, Farm Security Administration, July 1941. Library of Congress, Prints & Photographs Division, FSA/OWI Collection [LC-DIG-fsa-8a16024].

4

"Right Tight, Right Unruly"

Interiority and Wish Images

I would like to have a room all to myself with a desk and a lamp in it and anything I need. Well maybe someday I will have what I want. Miss Lee I love you and always will.
—Fourteen-year-old Susie Morgan, Southwest Washington, DC, January 3, 1939[1]

When I sit down long enough to imagine things, I think of day dreams of the success I'll be some day. Of the fine things I've always wanted, but most of all that I've seen the world.
—Fourteen-(or sixteen)-year-old James Albert Gray, Southwest Washington, DC, 1938[2]

Interviewer Laura Lee made her first visit to Susie Morgan's Clarks Court Alley home on May 5, 1938. She spoke with Susie's father, Oscar Morgan, a short, thin man in "worn overalls" who worked seventy-two hours a week as a dishwasher.[3] Lee told Mr. Morgan she had come to meet Susie's parents so that she could "understand [her] better," which was protocol for Frazier's study: to interview parents, grandparents, and siblings of the selected adolescent subjects. Oscar Morgan, surrounded by many of Susie's younger siblings, Clara (twelve), Freddy (nine), Charles (seven), Lillian (three), and the baby Mike, described his daughter Susie as "right tight, right unruly." When Lee asked specifically what Oscar meant by the word "tight," he responded, "hard-headed and overbearing." Lee commented that Oscar ought to talk to Susie. Oscar said that he couldn't because "she [was] *that* tight." Susie, he said, "cuss[ed] and [. . .] smok[ed] a little," although he was quick to add that she did not cuss at him. This same characteristic of "tight" is what Oscar said his wife was with their kids, and what Susie attributed to herself and her group of friends, crediting it for their ability to elude the police in all their points of contact with DC law enforcement.[4]

When Susie got back from school that afternoon and found Lee at her home, she was very displeased, asking, "What you come here for, Mrs. Lee?" Susie had been slightly dishonest about where she lived, identifying her address as 336 C Street (a main street address) instead of the alley address of Clarks Court. One afternoon she had also stopped Mrs. Simpkins, the social worker at the Southwest Community House, with whom she had a close and friendly relationship, from a home visit.

The fourteen year old had made a strong impression on twenty-one-year-old Laura Lee. After nearly a year of interviews that had started sometime in the early spring of 1938, Lee began to feel discomfort with interviewing Susie. Lee wrote a six-page statement sometime at the end of the year where she admitted that "the continuance of the contact with Susie [was] no longer for the purpose of the study, for to continue to try to interview Susie would be exploitation." Lee maintained contact with Susie, though, because, as she said, she "was interested in the child." And Lee kept "notes of the contact" for their "incidental value" to the study, evidently turning them over to Frazier, since they can be found in his papers.[5]

Susie also became very attached to Lee and her family. She wrote to, called, and visited Laura Lee in her Northwest parents' home, spending many evenings with them. Lee's mother is noted to have altered hand-me-downs for Susie to supplement her wardrobe in the winter of 1938–39, just as Susie's mother was about to give birth and her sister Dorothy was in the hospital with appendicitis.[6] Susie shared with Lee her frustrations with her family situation, her desire to leave home but her concerns about leaving her mother, her regret that her growing familial responsibilities meant that she missed considerable school, her difficulties getting to activities at the Southwest Community House (her fears of going "under the Railroad underpass [where] a man had chased her once"), and her need for a "desk with a light" to do her homework. She joked about quitting school altogether, from which Lee tried to dissuade her, saying "all [Susie] would be able to make [would be] $5 a week." Susie thought, though, "that was better than nothing." As Myron Ross did with Harry Stack Sullivan, Susie Morgan took advantage of Laura Lee's concern and attention to not only express her thoughts, beliefs, and desires. She also tried to improve her living conditions and put something in motion for a future she could already imagine. Susie had grown very fond of Lee, as is clear from her expression of love above in one of her letters to Lee.

Susie's narrative exemplifies the complex identities poor and working-class African American young people formed in interwar DC, as well as their deep consciousness of both the realities of Jim Crow segregation and of themselves as authorial subjects. While Susie's is one of the more comprehensive of the interviews, her narrative is not exceptional. She expressed many of the same views and self-reflective abilities her contemporaries did. "Youth" is constituted in processes, has been and is (naturally) associated with immaturity, and often it has been used to indirectly or directly indicate an absence of agency, of particular kinds of citizenship, and of the cultivation of intellectual life, all traditional signals of maturity. What comes through in the following narratives of quotidian and inner lives are ways in which young people understood themselves in and out of the context of their restricted Jim Crow realities. In addition to political ideologies shared in the last chapter, here narratives bring into relief racial identity formation; burgeoning notions of gender identity, femininity and masculinity; and, most importantly, imaginings for their futures. All of these helped poor and working-class young people navigate, negotiate, and defy the various forces of oppression and exploitation in interwar Washington, DC, delegitimizing, as much as they could, the systemic racial segregation and violence in which they lived.

In the early summer of 1938, self-identified sixteen-year-old James Gray sat in the Bell School Auditorium engaged in conversation. James likely knew his interviewer well. Dennis D. Nelson had been "the Boys Worker" at the Southwest Settlement House for two years, and James lived just down the street from the settlement house, stored many of his handmade clay figurines there, and was the secretary of one of the community center's sponsored programs. James's comments that open this chapter came in response to the following questions: "When you imagine things to yourself, what do you think about? What would you do if you had $100 to spend just as you pleased? What would you like to be doing ten years from now? If you could have one wish, what would it be? Did you ever wish you were dead or not born? When was that?"

From his answer, we get the sense that James had a very active life, for he often did not, as he said, "sit down long enough to imagine things." However, when he did, he certainly had musings, and they were on his future—one that included world travel and "fine" material things. But James also had a very pragmatic component to his response: specifically, he would buy "a bicycle, some clothes, and [he would give] part [of the $100] to [his] mother." On second thought, though, James realized the "trip" he would take would only be "at least as far as" the amount would allow, so maybe not quite around the world. For that, he said, he would need "plenty of money." Finally, in ten years James "hope[d] to be a successful physical education teacher."[7]

The census recorded tenth grader James Albert Gray as fourteen at the time of his interview, not sixteen as James said. The Randall Junior High School student, briefly introduced in the previous chapter, may have inflated his age, as he saw himself as the man of the house since the death of his veteran native Washingtonian father. James shared his Southwest home with his widowed Maryland-born mother, Pearl, and younger sister, Helen.[8] Described by Nelson as "a thick set black Negro boy with kinky hair" and with a "deformity, a thick tongue which makes talking difficult, as he talks with a lisp," James was also "witty, congenial;

playful; a good sport; a leader in his set and a cooperative individual in whatever group he [found] himself."

James got along well with both boys and girls, according to Nelson. Recently, a group of girls, which included his sister, working on a community newsletter, had "chosen [James] to head the club." James's narrative is one centered on his burgeoning awareness of his own masculinity, informing his role in his family and in his community of peers. The ideas articulated in his interview also call into question E. Franklin Frazier's assessment about the lack of literacy and lack of opportunity for leisure activities outside of extralegal ones, specifically in Southwest DC.

According to James, what Nelson described as James's affability was the result of his "deformity." "I was born tongue-tied," James said in response to an undocumented question. James had never been especially "aggressive." Because of his speech impediment, James had thought that "silence at the right time [was] the mark of a good leader." But, really, he found that his reticence had turned into "meekness," and "that alone added to [his] troubles." When he was younger, his passivity had resulted in "few enemies, because [he] wouldn't quarrel." But eventually, James was "thrown with a bunch that took advantage of this weakness and cheated [him] out of many things." He had "got[ten] to the point where [he] felt inferior to other boys." "When I played games," he said, "I was usually the last to be chosen and the first to be 'benched' when a better player came along. They told me I was good for my size." But one day, James said, "things changed!" That day James, self-described as 5'10" and 145 pounds (a description corroborated by Nelson), "tore into a boy who had been meddling with [him]." Two things happened, according to James: the bully got the shock of his life, and James gained a new perspective on himself. He realized he had grown "bigger and stronger than many of [his] tormenters." "From that day on," James said, "I assert[ed] myself to everyone and [held] the respect of all. I was chosen leader of my club and captain of some of the teams, and I've enjoyed the position ever since." So, while James did not run with a bunch, respecting his mother, who did not "approve of gangs," James certainly valued a show of aggression and strategically placed uses of force.

James's new abilities and the new respect he garnered placed him in leadership positions that had previously been closed to him. James belonged to the Southwest Community House–sponsored Southwest Junior Athletic Club, of which he was the secretary. He shared leadership with his neighbor Norris Klinkscale. James described the group as "about 15" who "nominate and vote on officers once a year." The criteria for "selecting" a "leader" was "the ability to do the job and on the confidence [the others had] in him." Once in the club, a member was held to a strict social contract, and if he did not "conform to the wishes of the officers" he had helped to elect, he was summarily "dropped." So in contrast to Nathaniel Smith, from whom we will hear later, who had been beaten up at the hands of Norris Klinkscale, the members in the Athletic Club, including James Gray, had democratically elected Norris as president and had kept him on because, as James described Klinkscale, he was "a quiet sort of fellow" who "everybody like[d], [. . .] a good athlete and always fair."[9]

Young James was also captain of the basketball team. He had helped form a baseball team and he belonged to the Guidance Club at school, where they played "soft ball, volley ball, and other playground sports, and a representative group always compete[d] in inter-school meets." Nelson described James as "a good athlete." He had received "numerous trophies" and took "great pride in the care of them." Nelson also wrote that James was "boastful, of course, but [could] prove his worth if put to the test." Although when James boasted of his prowess at Ping-Pong, Nelson and he "play[ed] a short match, [at Southwest House] which [James] subsequently lost, with," according to Nelson, "no alibis offered."

In James's musings on his affiliations we see the centrality of the development of institutional and community life among black teens. This work to build black institutional life has been identified as evidence of both a desire for and practices of racial uplift, black agency, and black resistance, as well as the realities of prohibition from engagement in

American institutional life more generally.[10] Here, as James Gray displayed his leadership abilities and was in turn rewarded with positions of authority, and as he and his peers enacted their democratic electoral capacities in the Southwest Community House's Junior Athletic Club, we see the primacy of rank, status, structure, and defined roles and responsibilities in black young people's social engagements, even those young people identified by social science as inadequately prepared by their parents and culture for full participation in modern (urbane) society.

Although James was incredibly social and "fun-loving," like Myron Ross, out of respect for his mother's wishes, he had not joined a "bunch or gang." James's Southwest residence put him in close proximity to both the youth-formed social club, the Society Gents Club, and a more raucous "bunch." But James saw them as more trouble than they were worth. He certainly associated with others who were in gangs or had a bunch, like Norris Klinkscale, for example. Still James did not see "where running in a crowd [would get him] anywhere." "Furthermore," he posited, "the more of a crowd one runs in, the more likely he is to get into trouble." If one "boy in a bunch" is arrested, James said, the police will then "have their eyes" on all members of the bunch "at all times." His beliefs about joining a bunch, though, did not prevent James from hanging out around the Columbus Fountain at Union Station or in parks or going to a show with "two or three *nice* boys [his] age" (emphasis added).[11]

James "practically live[d] at the [Southwest Settlement House]," but because it was "only a few doors" down, there were "no objections [from his mother . . .], as he was exceedingly helpful to the Center." According to Nelson, the young widowed Pearl Gray, who worked as a "domestic," was "glad to have both children in Settlement activities." James said it had been eight years since his father, a former enlisted man who had been "badly shot up" during World War I, had been "killed in an accident." James felt "sorry" for his mother, who he believed had "had an awful job" of having to raise him and his sister. He felt he "owe[d] it to her to get all the education [he could], [and] then get out and go to work."[12]

"Sober, honest, and exceedingly frank," James did not "mince words and frequently [found himself] in bad with the workers of the Settlement House because of his frankness," wrote Nelson. One gets a sense of James's candor and forthrightness in his response to what appears to be Nelson's question about what books James enjoyed and whether he enjoyed the moving pictures. James liked both "adventure stories and adventure movies"; he saw them as being morally innocuous. He also wondered why "they [didn't] show pictures of the things our people have done[:] pictures of what they did in the war (no doubt here thinking of his father), things they've invented, lives of men [like Joe Louis]." Movies with "all that slush and love-making hooey," James believed, just made his friends not only "try to imitate what they [saw] but to out do it." The fourteen year old did not think "movies of such kinds ought to be shown [to] young children."[13]

James followed this with a castigation of the bad behavior of his male peers, maybe here referring to the activities of his neighbors Joseph Knight, William Wright, Nathaniel Smith, and Smith's older brother: "The boys [who] used to take girls up to the Fountain at the Capitol just opposite Union Station, staying up there till late hours at night." But James was pleased that the "police [had] got[ten] wise [. . . and had] broken up that playhouse!" He described in detail the ways the cops patrolled the area, "shining their torches through all the bushes and picking up all they saw under the bushes or loitering around them." In James's view, this behavior had many causal factors: he blamed it partly on the negligence of schools, church, and parents in not "teach[ing] sex matters and the evils that ignorance of such things bring." So despite the emergence of sex education in schools in the early twentieth century, it was not prevalent, for many young black people, including James, lamented its absence in their schools. And, clearly, James also placed some blame on popular culture.

Finally, James shared Frazier's concerns about "salacious types of reading matter."[14] He blamed "sex magazines with bad stories [and] naked women" for "much of [this] trouble." James's sister, Helen, one year younger than James, so either fifteen or thirteen depending on whether James accurately self-reported or the 1940 census is correct, "[kept] her head buried in [these kinds of magazines] till they [were] read through." In general James did not think such reading material was appropriate for any boy or girl, but this after all was his sister and he did not "want to see her messed up," bringing "disgrace" on both "herself and the family." Here, as before with his articulation of the ways in which the racy content of some moving pictures made his peers want to "imitate" what they saw, James was concerned that the content of his sister's magazines would somehow necessarily lead her down the wrong path, and she would end up sexually active, consequently pregnant, and likely unwed. When he found he had no power to stop her from reading them, he told his mother, who "took them away and threatened to whip her if she brought in any more." However, Helen continued to read them, hiding them under her mattress, which James found, likely because he was looking. Again he took this evidence to his mother, who, much to James's chagrin and satisfaction, "sure did try to kill Helen about them." While James did not "like to see [his] sister whipped," he was certain that "such things," the reading of this kind of literature, could "lead to disaster," and so he continued alerting his mother to his sister's seemingly dangerous behavior, like the times he saw her "hanging around corners with boys and girls who [he knew were no] good for her." Proudly, James proclaimed that his mother always "[went] down and [brought] her back."[15]

Surprisingly, given the position James had taken on at home, as that of the male protective head, which often resulted in Helen bearing the physical and emotional brunt of her family's fears about her future, Helen had not refused her brother's participation and leadership role in her editorial club at the Settlement house. Despite James's attempt at being man of the house, or his newly developed and recognized physical prowess, he did not have clear enforcement power, certainly not to drag

Helen home from the corner or stop her from reading the increasingly popular magazines being produced for young adults and teens at the time.[16] James had to turn instead to his mother for enforcement.

James's sports and group activities showed him to be extroverted, but his exposition on the causes of youth delinquency revealed he had a contemplative side as well. Moreover, it was not a side of himself with which he was unfamiliar—he credited his experiences with "country life" at "camp" with "learn[ing] something of God in nature." He had found it "thrilling to lie out under the stars and *think*" (emphasis added), reflecting on "swell times," his future, and of traveling the world.

Camp had also given James his "first taste" of crafts. Nelson noted that James was "quite adept in the use of tools." During his interview, James "insisted" that Nelson accompany him to his home "to see the numerous products of his labors, and to the Center to see the results of his art study," which Nelson did. At home, Nelson saw pieces of wooden furniture and ornaments made by James scattered around the generally "ill-furnished six-room brick house." These included "tables, taborets, book ends, chairs, [a] buffet," all of which James said he had "made for [his] mother." Actually, James had made all of the furniture in the dining room. At the Southwest Settlement House, Nelson saw clay figures: "an elephant, a football player in crouched position," a baseball player, and James's most prized piece, "a much carved jewelry box" he had hidden "in an antiquated ice box." James's "eyes glistened as [Nelson] examined each piece and admired the workmanship." Nevertheless, James felt it necessary to disclaim his work: "I could have made better pieces," he said, "if I could have had better wood." Much of this had to be done with scraps. Someday, I hope to have tools of my own and I'll buy wood and make such things right here."[17]

Young James had decidedly stepped, at least partially, into the role of man of the house. Articulating a level of maturity in terms of his opinions on the causes of what he saw as the bad behavior of his sister and his peers, and in terms of his capacity for reflections on his own personal gender identity evolution and his consciousness, James was a complicated young man. A blossoming social butterfly, James reflected an intricate understanding of the importance of a strong physical presence in the performance of a socially accepted and respected manhood. He and his sister were both avid participants in sanctioned recreational activities, and yet James still saw Helen as at risk, and like other young people interviewed, he had made a deliberate decision to not be affiliated with a "gang" or a "bunch."[18] James could have merely been performing a particular kind of masculine maturity for Nelson; still, his ability to do so is notable. Because he had seemingly internalized normative gender roles and expectations, he did not fully lament, nor did he try to prevent, the abuse his sister Helen endured for what both he and his mother saw as transgressive and risky behaviors. (And, unfortunately, there are no interviews with Helen.)

For most of the young people interviewed, identity (racial, class, gender, sexuality) was in formation. Despite this, James and others seemed very aware of and could articulate how they saw and experienced these intersecting aspects of themselves. There is little that is necessarily pathological about these developments. Frazier assessed James's use of aggression as a result of his frustration with his racial and class position. However, James and the other young people's performance and ideologies about their gender identities and sexualities were on par with early twentieth-century cultural norms.

For the poor and working-class black young men interviewed, a burgeoning sexual and gender identity was framed at the time by both white masculinist notions and developing New Negro black masculinities. It was an admixture of a "'rough' code of manhood," in Gail Bederman's words, built on "aggressiveness, physical force, and male sexuality," and a "modern black masculinity," to borrow from Martin Summers, that included sexual activity, "unrespectable modes of leisure," political activity, and a desire for "access to mass consumer culture."[19]

(Oswald) Stanley Russell's interview also highlights the complicated interior life of coming of age in Depression-era Jim Crow DC. Stanley was fifteen and lived about 170 feet to the east of James Gray at the corner of E and Second Streets, closer to the Southwest Community House. A peer of Myron Ross Jr. at Armstrong High School, Stanley lived with his grandparents, Louise and William Coleman, his sister, Audrey (seventeen), cousin Lelia (nineteen), and occasionally his uncle and namesake Oswald Coleman. Frazier categorized Stanley, like James Gray, as "lower class." Dennis Nelson described Stanley's family as a broken one: Stanley and Audrey were "children of divorced parents," being raised in an unconventional household headed by their grandparents, a household that sometimes included uncles and cousins; they had little contact with their mother, a full-time teacher in the Virginia school system who worked all summer as a domestic in Atlantic City, or with their father, a Pullman porter who "did not support them," although he lived not far away in Southwest.[20]

Described as "very dark, stubby, with blunt Negroid features, [. . .] a devilish twinkle ever in his eyes, [. . .] very white teeth, [and] a pleasing smile," Stanley, according to Nelson, "dresse[d] neatly but not well." Despite the lack of convention, which for Nelson and Frazier was evidence of family disorganization and dysfunction, Stanley, like his mother, aunts, and uncles, had learned to play the piano under his grandparents' supervision and, as a result, Stanley was interested in "specializ[ing] in music" once he graduated from high school. "Between chords and runs on the keyboard," Stanley articulated his engagement with his own burgeoning identities and his sense of his future possibilities, despite both racial and class limitations.[21]

Stanley was "agile but lazy," Nelson said. He had "the physical appearance of a much younger boy, [and] act[ed] like one, but [thought,] however, that he [was] a man," despite "still wear[ing] short trousers." Not much of an "athlete," Stanley was "usually shunted about when a game with other boys [was] in progress." To the other boys, Stanley was "just a punk." But in his dialogue with Nelson, Stanley shared a strategy he had devised to deal with this. Stanley, in Nelson's words, was "ever striving to gain recognition through his antics." He was "the clown of his gang": "mischievous," "meddlesome," and often in fights.[22] Faced with the challenges of a seemingly late growth spurt, Stanley was experimenting with a social niche for himself as a bit of a troublemaker and a cut-up, taking the sometimes physically brutal consequences of being beat up by other boys in order to fit in. Even so, he still thought of himself as "a man," having found a way, if temporarily at least, to compensate for both his small stature and his short pants.

Despite still sartorially a boy, Stanley made use of his male privilege in the household. His older sister Audrey and older cousin Lelia, both also students, did much of the housework and cooking. The girls' comings and goings were highly supervised by their grandparents. In contrast, Nelson noted that Stanley "managed to slip through his grandparent's close scrutiny, roam[ing] as much as he [saw] fit." Stanley commented on this, too, saying that although he was expected to "help" with the housework, he was naturally of little help: "I guess I was just born tired."[23]

Stanley was a self-avowed city boy, having only been to camp once. Critical of the food—"beans on top of beans"—and generally unhappy about bats in his tent and snakes that "walk[ed] around like people," Stanley insisted he could only tolerate at most "an overnight hike," to which he would have to bring his own food. He was more interested in showing Nelson the car he had made for the upcoming soapbox derby. Once in the backyard with Nelson, Stanley was not sure his "de-luxe model [would] get by the judges," or that he would even be able to get it out of the yard; Nelson noted it looked as if it weighed 500 pounds at least. Its design was intricate, a hodgepodge of materials: "the body itself [was] a motorcycle side car with an elaborate canopy top." There were "seats, brakes, and even an instrument board," "heavy iron wheels, [and] a [full-size] steering wheel." Stanley admitted he was "no good at crafts or carpentry," that he had been thrown out of his hobby club for "wast[ing] good materials." Nelson "praised Stanley's workmanship despite the desire to laugh," but Stanley thought that if he could get it out of the yard without "having to tear it down," "she [would] do some real speed once she's started."[24]

Sponsored by the Chevrolet Dealers, the *Evening Star* newspaper, and the American Legion, the Soapbox Derby took place that July, in spite of rainy weather. While there is no record of whether or not Stanley Russell entered his car, fourteen African American boys participated, and a few of them placed first in multiple heats. Frazier's only white researcher, Ruth J. Bittler, attended the event, withstanding the heavy downpours, which suspended the race several times. Bittler informally interviewed black American Legion member Clifton Anderson, asking why more African American boys were not entered in the race. Clifton and his two friends responded in unison: "economic conditions. It's hard enough getting money for food, let alone building cars." Bittler learned that some of the white boys' cars had been built by their family's black chauffeurs. One boy had even been recently taught to drive by the family's chauffeur for the race after his car had been built.[25] While Stanley had a clear assessment of his skills as a hobbyist, it had not stopped him from devoting a considerable amount of time, skill, and energy to the building of his derby wagon, of which he was very proud. Similarly, despite what Frazier judged as Stanley's family disorganization and lower-class status, Stanley's grandparents owned their Southwest home and piano lessons had been an integral part of both their children and grandchildren's upbringing, so much so that Stanley imagined a future where he could "specialize" in music rather than a "regular academic college course."

E. Franklin Frazier was particularly concerned about the development of a malformed identity among young black people. Of the young people so far highlighted here, Frazier found reason to identify ways in which their personalities and their temperaments had been retarded and marred by racial segregation, by their "lower class" conditions, and, in some cases, by their migrant parents' status and cultural practices. Frazier thought one remedy could be engagement in sanctioned recreational activities. In his estimation, and that of other reformers, this would necessarily decrease the likelihood of what was thought of as juvenile delinquency. Frazier concluded that there was a relationship between socioeconomic status, family structure, gender identity, and sexuality development, and participation in a "gang." The question "What gangs or clubs do you belong to?" had particular significance in the study.

In the interwar period and the Depression era specifically, all poor and working-class young people were considered at risk for juvenile delinquency, but black young people had the added factor of race that imposed upon them an essentialized criminality. In northern and midwestern urban spaces, African American young people, because of their perceived migrant status and their racial identity, were more often treated like juvenile delinquents and experienced higher rates of arrest. Using the same environmental models in which most sociologists were trained, police believed that migrants were prone to delinquent behavior because of their struggles adjusting to modern city life and because "traditional community-based controlling institutions [had not] transferred [well] to the new urban setting."[26]

In Frazier's unpublished report on "recreation and amusement among American Negroes," he stated:

> A large number of the lower class are idle and spend their time hanging about pool rooms, beer joints, and dives. Because of loose family ties and the number of unattached men and women in this class, sexual indulgence plays an important role in recreation. This is true of the youngsters as well as the adults since many come from broken homes and are without parental supervision.[27]

But many of the young people interviewed discussed participation in both sanctioned recreational activities and organizations, and participation in or adjacency to, or both, what Frazier called a "gang." Often, this dual affiliation was acknowledged and even approved of by parents as a necessary outlet given the living conditions and the constraints of racial segregation that most poor black families endured.[28] Frazier concluded the section above with an indictment of a particular youth group, saying "in a slum area of Washington, there was a club of young men which required a man be a 'pimp' in order to gain membership." The "club" to which Frazier was referring was a Southwest association, the Society Gents Club.

In the summer of 1938, the Society's Gents Club was led by Joseph Ward Jr. (seventeen), who was introduced in the previous section, and Hoyt Scott (sixteen) who were "president and vice president," respectively, of what Hoyt called a "small bunch of boys."[29] Ward lived at Third Street near the corner of E in Southwest, around the corner from the Southwest Community House. Unlike Hoyt's father, who worked as a construction "laborer," Joseph's father was a "messenger" with the Treasury Department and they owned the home in which they lived. Hoyt and Joseph were neighbors in Southwest, both categorized by Frazier as "lower class boys," despite the Wards' homeownership.[30] According to Hoyt, he and Joseph, along with five other young people, including sixteen-year-old Norris Klinkscale, who as we know from James Gray's interview was involved in other youth groups, had all "known [each other] nearly all [their lives]," and, in contrast to Frazier's portrayal, had formed the group "primarily for social purposes." That June, they had sponsored "a dance at the Community Center," which had been "far from a financial success." "Southwest girls and boys don't appreciate a nice dance," said Hoyt, who was a native Washingtonian, as were his parents. The club had charged "20 cents apiece or 35cents a couple," and Hoyt believed that the community had been "spoiled" by "5 cent dances." Thus, he lamented that "the crowd was small." Still, though, Hoyt was pleased they had "kept the dance as nice as [they had] planned" despite the low turnout.[31]

The members of the Society Gents Club ranged in age from thirteen to seventeen, paid dues and met regularly, and "even dress[ed] very much alike." They also "had an athletic program." In the last season, Hoyt recalled, they had "played the Police Boys Club in basketball and lost to them 28–13." They had won some of the games, but generally had had "a miserable showing." Hoyt could not exactly figure out what had gone wrong but guessed that their losses had been a result of lack of teamwork: "Everybody seemed to have been playing for himself." Nevertheless, they planned "to try again next year."[32]

The Society Gents Club had made a membership invitation to fifteen-year-old Nathaniel Smith. Nathaniel, though, was not sure "he could make the grade."[33] He lived at 139 F Street Southwest, after having been born not far away in Sullivan's Court, one of Southwest's alleys. While Frazier disparaged the Society Gents Club for its imitation of adult "sexual looseness," for Nathaniel to have been invited to join the Society Gents Club was an honor. "First, you must be a pimp" to be invited to join, Nathaniel said, and "of course [you had to] know how to dance and mingle in society." For Nathaniel the invitation confirmed for him that he had indeed come of age as a man; "pimp" signified a particular aspect of his own burgeoning gender identity. Nathaniel identified Norris Klinkscale as "the *big shot* in that club," saying "if there ever was a *pimp*, it [was] him" (emphasis added), even if, as Nathaniel said, Norris did not actually "get along well with the girls 'cause he's too stuck on himself."[34]

Nathaniel did not like Norris much. The two of them had come to blows, and Norris had bested Nathaniel in a fight. Nathaniel said he was "waiting for [his] chance to get even, [because] when someone does something to [him, he] never forgets." Nathaniel's description calls into question what exactly he meant by the word "pimp." It is clear that membership in the Society Gents Club was a step up in (masculinity) status for him; his membership would also facilitate an opportunity for him to face Norris again and fully claim his manhood. Still, his description of Norris was a far cry from James Gray's praise of Klinkscale as a stand-up, well-liked fellow.

But Nathaniel had not yet accepted the invitation. He was concerned that he could not meet the sartorial standards of the group—most of the boys in the Society Gents Club got their new threads because, as Nathaniel understood it, their mothers bought them. He did not have a similar situation; rather, Nathaniel had to "scuffle around" for his clothes." And because of this, he did not want to "be embarrassed [by not looking] like the others." Nathaniel's mother, fifty-two-year-old Bessie Smith, a native Washingtonian, just could not afford it. Bessie worked as a "maid" for a "private family," as did her second oldest daughter, eighteen-year-old Clementine, who lived at home, along with Nathaniel's older brother, Edward, sixteen; his younger brother Wilbur, twelve; and his baby nephew. Each month, according to Nathaniel, Bessie purchased clothes and other necessities for one child and in the month prior to his interview, she had gotten some things for him, so, he thought, "it [would] be some time before [his] turn comes around again."[35]

Nathaniel resented his economic situation, saying, "Its [sic] sure tough being poor! And all the worse, if you're a poor Negro." Here, in Nathaniel's discussion of his concerns about his wardrobe, we see the close relationship between gender identity and bodily presentation, and the ways in which masculinity is performed: physically, relationally, and rhetorically: Nathaniel used the word "pimp" pridefully. Nathaniel also expressed his understanding of the impact of race on one's class position and the economic limits that prohibited young poor and working-class Washingtonians from participation in specifically conspicuous consumption, unlike their black middle- and upper-class counterparts.[36]

So, in the meantime, as Nathaniel built up his attire for the Society Gents Club, he "[ran] with a bunch of boys." This group included his older brother Edward; Joseph Knight, twenty-one; William Wright, nineteen; and Jack Harris, who Nathaniel named as "the leader." All of the boys hailed from Southwest and were neighbors. Nathaniel identified the necessary characteristics of Jack's leadership: Jack was "bigger" than Nathaniel, and "a lot rougher." Jack also had obvious skills with the ladies—he was a "pimp," though different from Norris Klinkscale. Although Nathaniel described Jack as "silly," he said Jack "sure [could] jibe girls. Before they [knew it] he practically [had] their dresses up." Jack had also been "chosen" as group leader because he was a mastermind for the group's extralegal activities. Nathaniel said, "We chose him because he's sly and a better liar than the rest of us, and he generally spots out the places beforehand . . . plans the get away, and the selling of the things we get." So like James Gray's explanation of the organizational structure of his sanctioned recreational group, selecting their leader based on appropriate skills, Nathaniel's bunch was similarly deliberate.[37]

Nathaniel excitedly related stories of their exploits: the time they "took all the electric fixtures out of a house and a gas stove" and, to Nathaniel's surprise, "got away with it," selling much of it for $8.00. The times they "took suit cases of packages out of cars and never got caught." He remembered they "used to wreck houses—go into empty houses and all we couldn't tear out to sell, we just tore up. Once we wrecked a Chinese Laundry, threw the iron stove and bed out of the windows, and took all the new screen doors to the place." However, Nathaniel was not able to benefit from the new screen doors at his own home because his mother Bessie would not have approved if he had brought one home; she "would have [had] a fit," Nathaniel said.[38]

Much as he might have enjoyed it, Nathaniel was clear that most of this behavior was in the past. It was not entirely his idea to give up this element of "fun," for he described himself as not "a patient fellow—I mean that when I want excitement I want it then." It was the reason he had not joined the Boy Scouts, for example. He thought most of those boys were "all a bunch of sissies." He had also refused to even join the Southwest Athletic Club, to which most of his friends already belonged. He did not "want to be with a dead bunch when [he] want[ed] fun."

The activities of his bunch had changed. The others were afraid of "getting caught" and being "sent to Lorton." Here Nathaniel referred to the Lorton Reformatory, located in what had been called Belvoir but was renamed Lorton, Virginia, and which in the late 1930s housed some 1,600 individuals convicted of criminal activities ranging from "rape, arson, violation of the narcotic laws, armed robbery, burglary, automobile stealing, housebreaking and grand larceny, pandering, tampering with the United States mails, and forgery."[39] More importantly than fears of being arrested and jailed, though, Nathaniel's "bunch" had "decided to become pimps." Since they had "put on long pants" and started "run[ning] with girls," they had "stopped some of the rough stuff."[40]

Nathaniel described himself as pretty sexually active: "I used to have relations with [. . .] girls in the alleys, in old garages, in the parks, in somebody's yard late at night, and once I broke into Bell school to do it." Most of this activity he could not quite take full credit for, saying, "no use wasting time with girls these days. They generally know what they want and there's no use delaying in giving it to them." But he had recently learned about venereal disease in his last year in junior high school and was grateful to his brothers and "guys on the corner" for schooling him. Like Myron Ross Jr. though, Nathaniel wished he had gotten sex education "in school or from [his] parents." Even though he "wouldn't have learned as much," at least, he thought, he might have been safer sooner. Like Myron, Nathaniel expressed frustration with the ways in which he had learned about sex and sexual health.[41]

Nathaniel took the opportunity offered by Frazier's project and Nelson's attentive ear to expound on his sexual activity, listing many places he had had sexual experiences with girls. In contrast to this performance, Nathaniel's interview also hints at his lack of experience and knowledge—that girls' desires seemed more in control of these interactions, and that new information about sexually transmitted infections was both welcomed and late. To Nelson, Nathaniel might have been prime data for both the impact of a "broken home"—Nathaniel's father, while listed as a resident in the home in 1930, by 1940 was seemingly not an official member of the family unit—and the notion that a lack of involvement in sponsored and supervised sports and other recreational activities led to Nathaniel's participation in illegal enterprises.[42] And this may well have been at least partly true. While Nathaniel makes it clear to Nelson that both the Southwest Athletic Club and the Boy Scouts were options for him, that many of his friends belonged to the former and encouraged him to join, but that he *chose* to spend his time otherwise engaged, it may be that, like his concerns about joining the Society Gents Club, Nathaniel was actually financially *unable* to participate in either the Southwest Athletic Club or the Boy Scouts. Both of those required membership fees or at least would bring costs for uniforms or other necessary equipment. Nathaniel stated very clearly in his interview that he "seldom [had] the money" to participate in any leisure activities, including the local theaters, except on Thursdays when there were free tickets. So what Nathaniel articulated as choice—his assessment of the Boy Scouts as less than manly and thus "a dead bunch"—might have actually been a statement on the lack of affordable, free, recreational opportunities for black poor and working-class youth, which would have bolstered Frazier's argument had he read it as such.

Joseph Knight was also a member of the bunch with which Nathaniel ran. Older than most of the young people interviewed, Joseph was twenty-one years old and lived next door to Norris Klinkscale on Delaware Ave between H and G Streets, just south of, and not yet cut off by, the 395 highway from the Southwest Community House. He corroborated Nathaniel's description of their group's adventures, foregrounding the kind of "rough stuff" Nathaniel mentioned. Joseph and the bunch "seldom traveled together as a whole gang," he said. Out of the fourteen members, there were never "more than three or four of [them] together" at one time. This segmentation might well explain why it was that Nathaniel Smith identified Jack Harris as the leader, while Joseph Knight saw William Wright as the leader, albeit for similar reasons that Nathaniel named Jack: William was "the biggest and the slickest too," according to Joseph. They never planned any of their activities in advance, Joseph noted, but rather would "roam around the neighborhood getting into everything in sight, making nuisances of [themselves]." They "broke in stores, stole automobile accessories, [and] took what was at hand. [. . .] a couple of foglights or a tire off somebody's car or a suit case or clothes out of another." Or they would "steal up a breeze" at a grocery store while one of them "bought a bottle of pop or something." But it was not until they "once tried to rob a man" that the police noticed them, and "stayed on [their] tails from that time on."[43]

In addition to burglary, they also went "to house dances and [tried] to break them up or just meddle[d] with women and girls on the streets." They "gambled, fought, and [were] arrested for both." There was "little

[they] didn't do," Joseph asserted proudly. However, like Nathaniel, Joseph noted that much of that activity was history. "I don't go in for any of that now," he said. Joseph's job limited when he could see and hang out with his friends. But that was not the only reason that he had stopped "running" with them. "The police," Joseph said, "[had] just about ruined the bunch. Now that [they] know us and keep an eye on us, we don't have much fun anymore." The group had "decided to quit before somebody got killed."[44]

Joseph's remarks on "meddling" in the above quote alludes to what will become clear later in his interview is actually sexual violence that he and his friends perpetrated. Young men and young women constructed their identities sometimes in collaboration with each other, and at other times antagonistically, as we'll see again with young women's expressed resistance to marriage. Some boys and young male-identified people included "rape" in their descriptions of leisure and recreation activities. In these instances, it is hard to fully interpret boys' expressions. Even if they were merely performatively boasting, the use of the word "rape" is hard to ignore.

Joseph, like Nathaniel, talked about his experiences with girls, saying that what had been the most "fun" group activity was "catch[ing]" them. In the next sentence, his use of the word "rape" is jarring. "We used to catch girls around here and over in Northeast and rape them. I raped four or five myself," he reported, "and those I didn't, I later 'got it' with their consent." Joseph remembered one night in particular that they had "caught a couple of girls and you can imagine my surprise," he said, "when I found myself on [top of] Wright's sister. Boy did [William Wright] raise Hell. And [Wright] had helped [to] catch them up in an alley back of Willow Tree Playground."[45]

From this description and the ones given by James Gray and Nathaniel Smith about this group's activities, it is hard to know just how Joseph Knight was using the word "rape." That he says he later had sex with some of these girls with their "consent" may speak to the accuracy of the use of the word in the first place: girls might have felt afraid of refusing him later. Joseph may have also used the word in order to merely portray what he thought of as his sexual prowess and power, and these may not have been actual instances of sexual assault. Still, Joseph clearly knew that rape was not consensual, as he makes a distinction between sex with and without consent. Additionally, for Joseph, violence, and violence against women, was not unfamiliar in his understanding of his masculinity. He described "slapping" his white girlfriend "for ignoring [him] around her friends." She responded by threatening to tell her father and her other (white) boyfriend, and so Joseph decided to "let her alone."[46]

Like some of the other boys interviewed, Joseph's sexuality (if we can think of what he calls rape in this case as an aspect of how he thought of himself as a sexual person), and thus his masculinity, evidently included domination and aggression; he clearly felt comfortable enough to use the word "rape" to describe his sexual exploits with seemingly no shame, remorse, or fear of reprisal. Joseph and his group's activities manifested as rife with "rough stuff": violence of all kinds. Leisure and recreation included it, which is partly what made it "fun." Manhood and masculinity were complex and could embody violative brutality.

Regardless of the ambiguity with which the word "rape" might have been used by young men interviewed, young black women were very aware of and alert to sexual and other kinds of violence and the fear of both in Washington, DC. Local newspapers featured stories regularly about violence generally and sexual violence specifically against black women and girls, by a range of perpetrators including DC police officers. As described previously, young women navigated spaces hypervigilant of physical dangers posed, mostly, by men, white and black. Girls like thirteen-year-old Rosella Hillman understood sexual assault to be very real. A boy had threatened Rosella with it after she had turned him down. She was afraid to be out late at night, fearing that "a man might grab me like they do some girls." Rosella also knew other girls who had been "raped" by white men.[47] Susie Morgan, Alice Williams, and Esther Wright all discussed this in their interviews, articulating their concerns about traversing especially dangerous spaces, where they had experienced harassment. And as we saw, high schooler Hazel Hughes brought charges against her suitor and classmate who had attempted to rape her while on a date, and who had facilitated her gang rape by two other men. These experiences of fear and trauma from sexual violence and harassment, or knowledge of and proximity to this reality, informed young women's gender and sexual identities, and come through in answers to questions about marriage and relationships.

Young people saw "gangs," "bunches," and "clubs" as very different things, distinct in terms of the membership, structure, activities, and goals and aims of each kind of organization, whether formal or informal. In Frazier's material, he conflated the Society Gents Club with a "bunch" engaged in more rowdy or violent and criminal activities; he was not able to discern the nuanced particularities made by the young members or observers themselves. Additionally, many of the narratives above highlight the complex nature of adolescent sexuality and gender identity as these young men made sense of their own desires, their heterosexual sexual experiences, and their evolving concepts and practices of manhood, often constitutive of accepted and pervasive elements of rape culture.

Boys and young men were not the only participants in or organizers of "gangs" or "bunches." Susie Morgan had organized and ran with "the Union Street Sports," which had twelve members. Susie said the gang had formed out of necessity, to provide a protective collective, to keep themselves safe. While on an errand for "white people" down at the Southwest wharves, Susie explained, "some larger girls took some money from one of us and we couldn't do a thing," she said. "So we decided to organize a gang." Susie was subsequently "chosen leader," for similar reasons that William Wright, Jack Harris, and Norris Klinkscale had been, because, in her words, she was "the best fighter." And she wasn't wrong. Earlier that spring, at a meeting of the girls' softball team fourteen-year-old Juanita Davis had complimented Susie on her mastery, saying she had overheard a boy at the fountain at Union Station tell another boy to leave Susie alone

Figure 4.2. Southwest girl. "Washington (southwest section), D.C. Portrait of a young Negro girl." Gordon Parks, photographer, Farm Security Administration, November 1942. Library of Congress, Prints & Photographs Division, FSA/ OWI Collection [LC-USW3–011073-C].

because "she can hit." And Juanita added, "you don't say anything, you just bip (making a sound of a blow)."[48]

Susie co-led the Union Street Sports with longtime friend Wilhelmina. Their mostly social activities included "giv[ing] nickel hops," sometimes stealing but not frequently, she said, and just hanging out. Like the Society Gents Club, the Union Street Sports was a dues-paying organization. Wilhelmina's aunt was the unofficial treasurer, and, like the Society Gents Club, Union Street Sports members also wore a "uniform." Members wore a "grey dress with a red braid on [the] collar" or blue skirts and sweaters.[49]

Despite the seemingly low level of criminal activity described by Susie, her bunch interacted with the police often. "The police," said Susie, "git after us a lot. But see, we so *tight*, they can't ever catch us." Here Susie described one of her group's favorite activities, that of "swim[ming] in the pool at the Lincoln Memorial," described in an earlier chapter. Ignoring police threats of violence, Susie and her friends appealed directly to Lincoln for access to the pool. Claiming this public, national space, Susie proclaimed not just adolescent defiance, although that is there, but also her identity as a citizen of the capital city with rights and entitlements, at least partly brought to her by the former antislavery president.[50]

Susie's activities with her bunch—traipsing across Southwest from the Lincoln Memorial Reflecting Pool to the Southwest wharves, to the Columbus Fountain at Union Station, fighting with boys, and running from the police—went against the behaviors Frazier thought of as appropriate for a young black woman. Frazier identified "the violent behavior" that included fighting, specifically with white people, as an indication of "deep-seated resentment and bitterness toward their lot in life," and as a result of racial segregation and its adherent economic privations.[51] But as we know from the opening narratives, this was not all there was of Susie Morgan, or other young people interviewed. Young people, despite participation in questionable recreational activities and the restrictions on their everyday lives, education, and employment possibilities, had dreams of the future.

For example, Myron Ross Jr., mobilizing Harry Stack Sullivan's interest in him, planned on going to Hampton Institute when he finished at Armstrong. His work with his father on the ham radio had given him lots of experience with electrical engineering and he hoped to pursue this. Sullivan had offered to help him achieve his college goal, inviting Myron to visit him in New York during the holidays, offering to put him in connection with Charles S. Johnson at Fisk University, and getting tuition together for him. Myron wanted to experience living in other places in order to assess whether his father was correct that DC was better. He wanted to marry "a brown-skinned girl," with a college education and some social skills. He wanted to have a "good job" and "to be some-body and to do something worthwhile." James Gray looked forward to becoming a physical education teacher and others saw themselves as military men or as professional people: teachers, nurses, secretaries.[52]

Susie Morgan's dreams stayed mostly within a traditionally gen-dered framework. She imagined being "a teacher's daughter," despite the improbability that either of her parents would become teachers. She dreamed of being rich, and of being a French teacher. But she also did not see herself as a wife, and instead wanted to be a "working woman," dismissing Laura Lee when Lee suggested she could be both. Susie was not a proponent of marriage. Even at fourteen, Susie felt she "had seen enough" to know marriage was not necessarily the best choice for a young woman. She cited her older sister who had a "real nice" boyfriend, but who, despite this, also did not want to "get married."[53]

Susie was not alone in her opposition to marriage. Fourteen-year-old Esther Wright also had little interest in the institution. Esther, who ex-pressed trepidation at being out late at night and fears of being accosted under the elevated railroad tracks traversing Southwest, may have also been the sister of William Wright who Joseph Knight had attempted to rape. (Wright had three sisters: thirteen, fourteen, and nineteen.) In Es-ther's third interview with Laura Lee in July 1938, she reported that she had a "boyfriend" with whom she had had sex for the first time some-time earlier that year. When asked, she said very clearly that she had "got no pleasure out of it." Esther was reticent about the sex questions, laughing through or trailing off in her answers to many of them, saying that she did not "fool with a lot of boys" as her way to prevent getting "diseases." But she was clear that she was not very interested in mother-hood, and in response to whether she "would like to marry this boy" she was seeing, Esther said, "don't care if I marry him, don't care if I don't."[54]

Lucy Savage, seventeen, whose living conditions and family were in-troduced in a previous section, expressed a similar opinion on the insti-tution of marriage. Lucy seemed in a particularly sour mood on the July day that Jean Westmoreland visited the small, dank one-room basement apartment she shared with her mother, her young son, baby sister, and younger brother. Westmoreland assumed Lucy was married, as she had a one year old, but Lucy corrected her. "I haven't got any husband," she said. "I don't want to marry him," referring to baby Yudell's father. Lucy thought her boyfriend had been "all right," but had never intended to marry him, even if he hadn't "got sick and had to be sent to a sanitarium." Adding, "I don't want to be bothered" with marriage.[55]

Lucy's comments about her disinterest in marriage were at least partly in the context of her answer to Westmoreland's question about whether she was seeing anyone. Lucy responded with a smile as she had done when Westmoreland had assumed that she'd had a husband. She said that she did not currently have a boyfriend, but she had had one. When Westmoreland asked her where he was, she said, "He's in jail," adding that she had put him there. Lucy's neck featured a long keloid scar "from her ear [to] below her chin [that went down to] her throat." She told Westmoreland how she had gotten it—that she and her friend Grace were on their way to Grace's boyfriend's house for dinner and Lucy's boyfriend did not want her to go. When she insisted on going, he "took out his knife and cut [her]." Because, according to Lucy, he was on probation for "larceny and theft," he was arrested and promptly placed in Occoquan.[56]

When Westmoreland tried to blame Lucy for the violence she had experienced at the hands of her former boyfriend, saying "You probably had been too intimate with him, had you not?," Lucy responded, "I guess that's the reason," but Westmoreland noted that Lucy's response seemed to "register no emotion."[57] Lucy's seemingly dispassionate response at this moment, when alternatively many teens knew and spoke their minds, and when up until this point in the interview Lucy had shared personal and no doubt traumatizing experiences, could be interpreted as a limit in Lucy's willingness to communicate. Lucy may have initially felt that Westmoreland's questions were an indication of concern or care, and Westmoreland's victim blaming may have triggered a protective emotional shutdown for Lucy, a culmination of a weariness from her interviewer's implied criticism and scrutiny. What we draw from Lucy's firsthand experiences with violence at the hands of her boyfriend, though, is a relationship between those experiences and her reasoned disregard of marriage. Here, Lucy was not alone.

Rosella Hillman was only thirteen when she was interviewed but she too was asked about whether she had a boyfriend. She and Laura Lee sat on the Howard University campus for what was their second interview in the summer of 1938. Rosella was described as outgoing, someone who loved to sing and dance, but her teacher found her dancing to be alarmingly flirtatious. Rosella's musings on marriage came after she had answered questions about her family, spending most of her time discussing her mother's current beau, Mr. Mitchell. Rosella (and her brother Winston) felt mistreated by Mitchell, and Rosella shared stories of mostly emotional abuse, especially when Mitchell had been drinking. She had two younger siblings, Mitchell's children, who, she said, Mitchell privileged over her and her brother. Rosella was so angry at Mitchell that in response to Lee's question of "what would you like to do most of all" (meaning in her life), Rosella twice responded that she would like "to bust Mr. [Mitchell] in the head and have him locked up."[58]

In the aftermath of sharing this information, Rosella insisted she did not currently have a boyfriend, nor did she want one, adding "I don't know if I will get married." She worried that if she got married her husband might try to control her, and then she "would get mad." Lee wondered if he would be able to control her, asking, "Would that stop you [from doing what you pleased]?" To which Rosella replied, "He might beat me." Describing a scenario not unlike Lucy Savage's, Rosella shared a story about a young married woman who had tried to "go to a dance" against her husband's wishes. Her husband waited for her to return and met her as she walked home alone from the dance and "beat her up." In Rosella's experiences, "some married people's lives aren't good."[59]

Fourteen-year-old Martha Harris too had stories of relationships gone wrong and did not want to "get married young." She wanted to continue school, "go as far as [she] can," and eventually train to be a nurse who took care of people in their homes, like the nurse who had visited her father several times since he had come back from the hospital. Martha also had two older brothers, both of whom were married, and she regaled Laura Lee with stories of each of their wives. In her opinion, one of the marriages would not last because her brother's wife did not seem to want to be married: she spent most of her evenings at the beer garden, and sometimes did not come home at night. While Martha's parents were still together, Martha's father had had numerous strokes and needed a great deal of care at home. Martha's mother took very good care of him, but Martha said that her mother also had a boyfriend.[60] Alice Williams too asserted that she wished to remain single. "Sick" and "tired of Washington," she wanted instead to "travel all around with a female [companion]," stating vehemently that she intended to "be an old maid."[61]

The above girls' disdain for marriage could be attributed to their youth, but members of an older cohort of young women also agreed. Anne Winston and Henrietta Belt were both in their early twenties and both were listed as members of a burgeoning domestic workers' trade union.[62] Anne had landed a Works Progress Administration job that required her to live away from home. She and her mother met up at an organizing meeting for the newly forming Women's Trade Union League, where Jean Westmoreland spoke with both of them. Anne too said she didn't want to be "bothered" with marriage "and all it entails," and she was equally indifferent to having children. She believed that her mother's bad decision, "marr[ying] the wrong man," in her opinion, had a negative effect on Anne's life—on her ability to go to school and achieve her personal and career goals—and Anne wasn't interested in making the same mistake.[63]

Henrietta Belt shared this disinterest. She was twenty-four when she was mistakenly interviewed. Not the intended "Henrietta," but rather the Henrietta at the address when the interviewer showed up, Henrietta Belt was the aunt of the intended Henrietta (Hinton). During an interview that lasted longer than researcher Jean Westmoreland expected and which she documented, but later drew an "X" through, Henrietta Belt discussed many things, including her decision to not get married. Henrietta worked as a live–in domestic. When she wasn't working in Chevy Chase, Maryland, Henrietta stayed with either her sister Carrie in Southwest (whose eighteen-year-old daughter was the intended subject of Westmoreland's visit) or with one of her brothers in Southeast.[64]

Henrietta, like the young women speaking above, discounted getting married, citing much the same reasoning as the other young women had. She said she had had many opportunities, and was even currently dating. Maybe because she was not Westmoreland's intended interviewee, Westmoreland challenged Henrietta on whether she had never been in love with someone and subsequently wanted to be married, and then on whether she had considered becoming a nun, for Henrietta had also spoken about her Catholic devotional practices. Henrietta reacted with conviction: she took pride in her single identity, the only one in her family who had not gotten married. She also did not see the point in marriage, noting what she knew of other people's married lives that included "fussing," "beatings," and a lot of "bother." Finally, she made it clear that while she did not see herself as married, given that she had both her "health" and a "job," and that she was used to "an independent life"; she also did not see herself as celibate and had never entertained becoming a nun.[65]

The choice to delay marriage (and motherhood) but not sex, in the Depression era, was not an anomaly. While the behaviors and notions of these young people could be looked at, and were, by sociologists and social reformers, as racially and economically specific to black poor and working-class young people, they were not that far from the national trends of young people generally during the interwar years and the Depression era. Premarital sex, for example, was pervasive among white college-aged young people. Young black women were part of this cultural shift, even if black reformers, invested in racial uplift and respectability politics, refused to see it, or, rather, saw it and read it as a problem. (Moreover, many of these young women's poor and working-class mothers had also delayed marriage and pregnancy.) But young black women and girls' articulations of their reasoning for opposition to marriage seemed to also be a response to and a rejection of the construction of a prescribed gender identity and role that required that their bodies be used in service to boys' and men's proof of masculinity.

Many young black men grappled with their understandings of themselves, navigating and negotiating with cultural norms about acceptable masculinity. Some looked to military enlistment to get out of DC, to travel, to rise in economic status, but also to prove their membership in a particular kind of manhood. They engaged in or postured engagement in violence against women and girls, property damage, and fighting. Some young women also participated (pridefully) in fighting and stealing, gesturing toward ways in which these behaviors were part of their developing gender identities. Young people wrestled with the intersections of race, class, gender, and age in the Jim Crowed capital, wondering if DC was really better than points south, given their experiences. Still, they imagined futures for themselves that allowed for possibilities outside of their current status, futures that included college, family life, fulfilling and enjoyable employment, along with adequate and secure food and housing.

Frazier's project sought to assess and access the inner thoughts and beliefs of black adolescents in order to prove that inferiority and hopelessness were environmentally produced by segregation and Jim Crow policies, especially among the poor, the working class, and newcomers from the rural South. While much of what he collected on this adolescent inner life does not appear in his publication, the voices of these young people are instructive. Their musings do not bolster Frazier's thesis that poor and working-class black young people felt themselves to be inferior. Certainly some young people, like Myron Ross Jr., expressed a desire to be white or lighter-skinned, while also articulating a very clear understanding and even "satisfaction" with the reality of their complexions. But the ability to imagine a future that both took into consideration the limitations of structural color prejudice and economic

discrimination and that transgressed the boundaries by the sheer nature of the existence of an imagined future, "a bright outlook on life," as
James Richmond had, highlights intellectual activity on the part of these
very young people.[66] These seemingly improbable visions of the future
were important "wish images"; while they might have been unrealis-
tic, they demonstrated that black poor and working-class young people
saw themselves as not just capable and deserving of, but maybe even
"entitled to, more" than they had at the moment at which they were interviewed.[67] Steeped in the contemporary psychological understanding
of adolescence as a "phase," these young black Washingtonians seemed
(maybe naively) certain that any teenage struggles they experienced in
the late 1930s would be overcome with time.

No transcript exists of seventeen-year-old Louise Freely of Southeast
Washington, DC, in Frazier's archives. Instead, what is left of Louise are
twelve poems she wrote in the summer of 1937. "My Book of Poems,"
"She Dreamed of Days Gone By," "Some One," and "I Know" are a few
of the titles. Louise's poems speak of love, of longing (for the telephone
to ring), of love lost, of daydreams, of a certain future (although she did
not know if it would be filled with love or heartbreak), and of the joy
writing brought her. We do not know whether Louise offered her work
up to her interviewer or whether she was asked for it, but either way her
young (artist's) voice can be found in this archive.

Neither Louise's poetic inclinations nor the musings of her inner
teenage self are referenced in Frazier's adolescent personality study publication. Rather, Louise and her cohort of young people were rendered
apathetic with a kind of social science violence of its own. Perceived
as mere victims of their parents' backward rural folkways, black poor
and working-class young people were depicted as overcome by urban
poverty and segregation, and thus had developed criminal, violent, promiscuous tendencies. But prioritizing interiority makes us take a second
look at what Louise has left us. Certainly, her words could be read as
typical teen angst, but they are also equally expressions of her introspective self, of meaning she is making about the world in which she lived.

Young people's articulated analytic frames help us to see the impact of larger, pervasive societal ideas. They found ways, some successful, others dangerous and disturbing, to navigate and make sense of their changing bodies, emotional lives, their quotidian experiences, and historical, political, and material realities. They took charge, sometimes aggressively and other times passively, of making possibilities for their futures, with an understanding that their adolescence was indeed fleeting.

Conclusion

The Detritus of Lives with Which We Have Yet to Attend

In January 1942, twenty-six-year-old African American photographer and musician Gordon Parks came to Washington, DC, to work with Roy Stryker at the Farm Security Administration as a Rosenwald Fellow. Upon arrival, an "excited and eager" Parks reveled at being in "this historic place." As he approached the city, he thought about "the White House, the Capitol and all the great buildings wherein great men had helped shape the destinies of the world." Parks saw his future work at the Farm Security Administration as building on the "tradition" of these men. He "felt their presence, [would] touch their stone, [and] walk under trees and on paths where Presidents had walked."[1] When Stryker sent him out to further explore the city on his first day, encouraging him to "go to a picture show, the department stores, eat in the restaurants and drugstores," to "get to know the place," Parks thought Stryker was being "trivial," but he humored him. Downtown, Parks stopped at a drugstore "for breakfast." Upon sitting at the counter, he was greeted by a white waiter with "get off that stool," and a command to "go around to the back door if you want something." At the theater, he had a similar experience, being admonished by the ticket seller that he "should know that colored people can't go in here." At this point in his day, Parks wondered whether this was all an elaborate prank by Roy Stryker, finding it "hard to believe" that there was "such discrimination in Washington, DC, the nation's capital." Finally, he went to Garfinckel's department store, whose "ads were always identified with some sacred Washington monument." He was sold a hat by a salesman he described as "a little on edge." Then, as he exited the store he saw an advertisement for a camel-hair coat, which he had always wanted. He took the elevator upstairs to the coat department with an incredulous elevator operator. The hat sale, Parks recounted, had "relieved his doubts about discrimination" in DC: his attempt to buy it had been partly an experiment. But the coat was the real thing. On the floor with coats, four idle salesmen ignored him. When he finally asked someone for help, he was sent to the coats on his own, to look for his size himself. When he insisted on getting their help, excuses were made and he was ultimately asked to wait, and after some small talk with a gentleman who said he was the manager, Parks was left alone on a couch and never attended to. Finally, he left the store, without the coat, which he said he would not have "accepted [even] if they had given him the entire rack."[2]

After several months in DC and experiences that included police harassment and witnessing police brutality and abuses of power, Parks decided that Washington, DC, "was not the place for my children to grow into adulthood."[3] Parks's surprise and anger at the stark contrast between his expectations of the capital city with its symbolic representations and the sometimes subtle and often hostile discriminatory practices and policies of individuals and places in the District, including the cafeteria in the federal building that housed the Farm Security Administration, is something Parks shared with the young people at the heart of this project.

A few years after Parks came and left the capital city for which he had had such high hopes, the report of the National Committee on Segregation in Washington, DC outlined many of these same incongruities.[4] It examined housing and job discrimination in the District, finding that overwhelmingly black Washingtonians were employed as laborers, domestics, or service workers, "while only one-eighth of white employees were in those categories." For African Americans, even in the capital city, there would be no Horatio Alger story: "a colored boy, no matter how ambitious, cannot hope to become a streetcar motorman." Black folks in DC faced exclusion from most skilled trades by craft unions, from other industries by management policy, including within city and federal government employment. The report noted that in 1938, when young black people were being interviewed in Southwest and around the city, many of their parents "were confined to the lowest custodial-labor status." "Colored people," the report stated, had "never recovered from the blow struck them" by President Woodrow Wilson's segregation policies in the federal government, which had and continued to "set an example of racial discrimination to the city and the nation."[5] "Segregation in employment [was] a form of bondage," asserted the report. It assigned "by color" African Americans to "the least desirable jobs" and consequently to "chronic unemployment," low wages, longer hours, and "poverty."[6] (Additionally, in 1939, when Marian Anderson performed at the Lincoln Memorial, after being denied space at both Constitution Hall and the local white high school, she was forced to stay in a private home for want of a hotel that accommodated black guests.[7]) The report concluded by identifying Washington, DC, as the "Capital of White Supremacy."[8]

President Harry S. Truman's executive orders 9980 and 9981, desegregating the armed forces and the federal government, followed closely behind this report, as did Truman's own Committee on Civil Rights' report.[9] Educator and activist Mary Church Terrell and Annie Stein, who was one of the organizers of the Women's Trade Union League of which interviewees Anne Winston and her mother both were members (see chapter 3), worked to end segregation in restaurants and other private businesses, leading the Coordinating Committee for the Enforcement of the D.C. Anti-Discrimination Laws. In 1953, the Supreme Court ruled in the *District of Columbia v. John R. Thompson Co.* that those laws were indeed legitimate and required enforcement.[10] A year later, in 1954, the Supreme Court decided *Bolling v. Sharpe*, the DC public school desegregation case about unequal middle school facilities in Southeast.[11]

The 1950s also saw Southwest DC's continued slow geographic and landscape shifts come to a head. Redevelopment generally of Southwest had always been imminent and some like Myron Ross's father, Myron Ross Sr., had seen it as being likely beneficial to his property values as a Southwest homeowner. In the wake of World War II with the end to the Depression era economy, the District finally allocated the funds for urban renewal in Southwest, which included the destruction of alley streets and the demolition of long-held homes and many of the community and communal spaces described in the pages above. Some 20,000 primarily African American families left Southwest as a result of the postwar urban redevelopment. A small percentage were able to be relocated in Southwest, but most moved to Southeast and Northwest, troubling both the few white and mostly middle- and upper-class black residents there.[12]

One study found that while some families were relocated with federal support into newly constructed, modern low-income housing, or were able to make use of, either through purchase or rental, homes that had been abandoned in white middle-class flight to the suburbs, most experienced the relocation as a loss. The housing folks left was in most cases "substandard"; often families, like Susie Morgan's or Lucy Savage's, endured filth, no running water, no electricity, and outhouse toilets. Still, while Southwest's black residents had been portrayed as generally transient, many were actually "firmly and well-rooted in their neighborhoods": nearly 65 percent had resided there for more than a decade, as was the case with several of the families in Frazier's study.[13]

Moreover, notwithstanding the new modern conveniences in many of the new homes and that most people "like[d their new spaces] very much more" than their "former house in Southwest," they had not only "strongly disliked having to move," many folks were also "very sorry [they] had to move." Others were glad for new sanitation and garbage collection services, but felt they had lost a certain "neighborhood spirit" and a sense of community. They were not convinced that their move had resulted in better neighbors, safer streets, or "more adequate police protection."[14] Residents who moved into public housing resented the rules and regulations of the National Capital Housing Authority—specifically that folks "could not plant their own flower seeds as they were used to doing in Southwest," or that they could not have the kind of company that they wanted, or pets.[15] So, while most former South-west residents were clear that their former homes were inadequate in providing basic amenities—like running water, sanitation, sometimes necessary shelter—the redevelopment of Southwest had resulted in "a social loss"; they had lost community and the feeling of protection for themselves and their children that neighborhood relationships, proximity to each other, and maybe even the containment of racial segregation had brought them.[16]

For African Americans, especially those in interwar Washington, DC, circumscribed not just by racial segregation but by political disfranchisement in the district, and for young people who, even if African Americans and District residents had had voting rights, would not have been old enough to engage in formal politics, articulating their sensibilities about local and hyperlocal, as well as regional and national, conditions and realities, was significant: an assertion of a critical self necessarily engaged in family, community, society, politics, and nation. *Coming of Age in Jim Crow DC* draws us into the interwar period to hear these voices in violent, turbulent, and pregnant times.

To do this, I drew on Saidiya Hartman's methodological approach to access the "detritus of lives with which we have yet to attend, a past that has yet to be done."[17] Hartman advises both "narrative restraint," to allow for unanswered spaces, for "what we cannot know," and "the imperative to respect black noise," expressions and representations that "exceed legibility and . . . the law."[18] Despite the ways in which New Negro intellectuals' work has been used to paint the culture of poverty theses and the origin of black ghetto narratives, researchers like Frazier entered into racial uplift and knowledge production about the black "masses" with a politics inclined toward racial justice.[19] In some places Frazier determined intelligence, temperament, and physical heredity as partly biological, but he also saw them as unfixed and influenced "by social interaction."[20] With an aim to implicate the at least partly psychological violence of racial segregation and economic discrimination, Frazier's study of black adolescent personality development in the 1930s assumed that personalities changed over the course of an individual's life and sought to prove the extent to which African American young people's "experiences" in the "isolated world" of Southwest DC had created "attitudes, traits, and evaluations" in an individual both about themselves and about the world.[21] More importantly, though, Frazier assumed that young people possessed an inner life and introspective capacities that would give him the data he needed through the ethnography of interviews. In his introduction to the 1967 edition of *Negro Youth*, noted sociologist and anthropologist St. Clair Drake praised Frazier for his ability to elicit "spontaneous and incisive comments" from the young individuals interviewed. Frazier's study assumed black young people's epistemologies, although he did not think of them in this way. But his (justified and necessary for the time) insistence on the structural and his focus on the material left him little room to recognize, let alone analyze, the wealth of answers his researchers documented.[22] His final publication actually ignored so many of the very experiences and conceptions of self that showed deep consciousness about and engagement in the community of life, the very "spontaneity and human interest" Drake praised.

Reading against and also leaning into the limits of these archives, I found that young poor and working-class black people took advantage of the listening ears and intrusive questions of their interviewers to articulate their own notions of everything, from "home" to white supremacy. These young voices named and claimed their subjectivity, their individuality, their memberships in communities small and large, their developing race, gender, sexuality, and class consciousness, and many of these young people looked forward positively. Through black poor and working-class young people's musings, we get a glimpse at a meditative and reflective, vulnerable space where (the social, the political) self is crafted, where "the practice of knowing is incomplete" and also constantly in formation.[23]

Examining the viewpoints of young black poor and working-class people in the late 1930s, outside of sociologists' determinations, leaves me wondering how they further activated and how these views evolved over time. I haven't yet found what happened to most of the young people featured in the narratives within these pages. There is some evidence that some of the young men enlisted as the US was entering World War II. I am still searching to answer my lingering questions. Were they displaced with their families from Southwest, or had they already left? More importantly, though, I wonder how many of these young thinkers, social and political critics, and space-occupiers, were later engaged in black DC's fights for equal access to housing, schools, jobs, restaurants, and voting rights that took place over the following thirty years. How many of them joined the picket lines at busy intersections and rallies in May 1943 to protest the city's bus company's resistance to hiring black drivers? Were they part of the Howard University students' sit-ins in early 1944 of Northwest restaurants, or the lobbying and petition drive to get a DC civil rights bill? How many of them kept their children out of school during the two-month school strike that started in December 1947 along with pickets of the Board of Education as the fight for educational access further heated up in DC?[24] What roles did they play in the Coordinating Committee for the Enforcement of the D.C. Anti-Discrimination Laws in the late '40s? After all, some of the young and adult women were members of or participants in the Women's Trade Union League of DC where they would have met and worked with Annie Stein. Stein and Terrell's 1949 Coordinating Committee helped to organize boycotts of racially discriminatory stores like Kresge and Hecht's.[25]

How many young people who were interviewed in 1937 and 1938 risked evictions to be part of tenant activism in early 1960s Northwest against landlords in violation of DC's housing codes? How many helped organize and participated in the "March for Freedom Now" in June 1963, weeks after Medgar Evers' murder, chanting "How long? How long?"[26] How many showed up on the National Mall they had watched expand or on which they had illicitly played to be present for the national March on Washington for Jobs and Freedom later that August? How many listened from the crowd of 250,000 to Marian Anderson's rendition of

"He's Got the Whole World in His Hands," to SNCC's John Lewis, and SCLC's Martin Luther King Jr.?

Did any of those who were forcibly relocated to Southeast later help to organize or join the Barry Farm Band of Angels or the Washington Welfare Alliance as antipoverty activists demanding a voice in urban renewal plans for Southeast?[27] Or, remembering earlier anti-police-brutality campaigns, how many were involved in testifying in late 1967 about police harassment, mistreatment, and other abuses of power in front of the newly organized city council of Washington, DC, and the later fight for community oversight of DC's police department? And what about the uprisings and the antifreeway activism: How many of the folks interviewed for *Negro Youth at the Crossways* were there as participants, commentators, or critics?

Remembering that our young people possess and are cultivating epistemological spaces is of critical importance now. As I began to fully understand this project, the Black Lives Matter movement emerged and solidified, coming out of the death of two young black people: Trayvon Martin and Michael Brown. Since then we lost a host of others through state and community violence. Media and other representations of many of these young people have been essentially pathological. Black girls and young women have been represented as "loud" or "threatening," especially when in a group, as sexual beyond their years, and sexualized. For black boys and young men, they are portrayed as threatening, whether together or alone, as dangerous, as criminal, and as Ferguson police officer Darren Wilson testified to about his shooting of Michael Brown, as aggressive, superhuman, and even evil.[28]

While these portrayals have origins early in our history, in our contemporary moment, with its social media capacities, the contrasts between who these young individuals actually were and the portrayals can often be stark. We see the continued ravages of the criminalization of black young people. Racial profiling of all kinds necessarily ignores, even denies, the existence of inner quiet, self-consciousness, of the dynamism of inner life, of a place of vulnerability, need, spirituality, intimacy. It negates the humanity of the one who is being profiled—all that is seen is their public self and the choices they have made for outward self-expression, the "narrow corners of social identity."[29] What were Michael Brown's wish images? What did he expect to find in college next year? What was he planning to major in? Where did he see himself in five years? What did Tamir Rice think of his new toy? What were his opinions on his teachers? How did Trayvon Martin compare the community in Sanford that he was visiting to his home in Miami-Dade County? How did he make sense of the differences and the similarities? What did Aiyana Stanley-Jones like most about school? What book had she read recently, and what did she think about it? What did she want to grow up to be? These are the kinds of questions asked of young people in the years before the US entered World War II that, despite the intentions of the sociological project, brought forth an epistemological trove. Interiority has its own geography: the meanderings of the mind on a range of issues and wish images that project across time and space into imagined futures. We will never know the answers to these questions for the above murdered black young people or hear how these young people were coming to understand the world in which they lived.

ACKNOWLEDGMENTS

In the late summer of 2011, my mother Ena Austin died. She was eighty-one years old, having been born in Bartica, a small market town on the Essequibo River toward the interior of Guyana, South America. She migrated to New York in her early forties with two grown daughters and two very young daughters, and for over twenty years worked as a live-in home health aide in Flatbush, Brooklyn. My mother's death, in the third year of my doctoral program just two months before I took my oral qualifying examination, fundamentally changed my life, my view of the world, and my cosmological understandings. I have since learned that the loss of a parent does this, regardless of one's relationship with that parent. It is a deeply disorienting experience and left me afloat and untethered—to both the conceptions and the materiality of "family," "work," "leisure," "memory," and history, the very thing in which I was being trained. Her death, despite our fraught relationship, left a gap that became filled with work. The narratives I crafted with the voices that sprang from a sociologist's 1930s interviews with mostly black women and young people in the developing and segregated capital city became in many ways the story of my mother, who migrated with her daughters from her rural upbringing to New York City for a better life, and the story of me—a first-generation immigrant coming to understand notions of home in a changing urban enclave.

Two years later, in the fall of 2013, unexpectedly, I lost my second mother. My dear, dear friend and mentor Pearl Shelby Sharpe had just the year before helped me facilitate the spreading of my mother's ashes into the Caribbean Sea. Pearl, who hailed from Compton, California, and who kept me grounded in Durham, North Carolina, was far more invested in the potentiality of a Professor Austin than I ever was. My

PhD was as much Pearl's project as it was mine. I knew I would finish my academic program, despite obstacles both professional and personal, because Pearl knew I would, and I would become the first person in my family to earn a doctorate.

These two women laid some foundations for me and I have many people to thank—from the iteration of this project to its completion.

Herman L. Bennett came into the History Department at the CUNY Graduate Center and became my mentor and advisor, and that could not have been better timed. His support, guidance, wisdom, feedback, and his time, energy, and commitment to my success are what sustained, and continue to sustain, me. Herman's attention to and investment in my project is what made me the scholar I am, although any and all errors herein are mine alone! The Herman Bennett–Jennifer Morgan household became my touchstone for much decision-making, and in many ways it still is. Without them, I would not be making it through the sometimes harrowing experience that navigating the academy can be for a woman of color.

Herman Bennett also introduced me to Clara Platter at New York University Press. And I have Clara to thank for her knowledge, guidance, counsel, and shepherding of this project through, for fielding my calls and questions, for her excitement, and for working with my schedule.

I am deeply indebted to Michele Mitchell, Gunja SenGupta, Robert Reid Pharr, and Clarence Taylor for their time, attention, and interest in this project, and their incredibly thoughtful and thought-provoking questions, comments, and suggestions. They were part of a profoundly smart, instrumental, and affirming dissertation committee (which Herman Bennett also made possible!). Michele Mitchell, since then, has served as an important sounding board and a continued source of support.

A special community of friends has provided the kind of camaraderie, guidance, and loving judgment, as we like to call it, that I continue to treasure. Lauren Santangelo, Logan McBride, and Thomas Hafer are the most wonderful people. I deeply respect their scholarship and trust their opinions and politics, and they have provided me with an inexplicable amount of love, rigorous feedback, laughter, reality checks, drives home, conversations about food and clothes, baked goods, and group texts. May those continue forever. I would be very remiss if I did not also thank Laura Hado and Thai Jones for their support and advice (and cookies), both actual and via the Santangelo–Hado and McBride–Jones teams.

I have been fortunate to have had the support of fellowships that not only helped to make it possible for me to complete this project but that also resulted in a community of people who gave me serious and thoughtful feedback on my work, and who acted as an advisory council of listening ears that I have definitely bent! Thank you to the Institute for Research on the African Diaspora in the Americas and the Caribbean at the CUNY Graduate Center: to Zee Dempster, Robert Reid Pharr, and Martin Ruck, and to members of my cohort, Ryan Mann Hamilton, Anne Donlon, and Christine Pinnock. Thank you for believing in this. And as the recipient of the Graduate Center's inaugural archival fellowship in partnership with the New York Public Library's Schomburg Center for Research in Black Culture, I benefited from the intellectual contemplation, wise words, reflections, and support of Jessica Krug, Devyn Spence Benson, Rafia Zafar, John Perpener, Rashad Shabazz, Myra Armstead, and James Smethurst. Farah Jasmine Griffin, Duncan Faherty, and Khalil Muhammad are scholars whose intellectual contributions I profoundly respect, and I feel incredibly honored to have had them as shepherds and facilitators of this project. My year in the Schomburg Scholars-in-Residence seminar was more valuable than words can possibly express here. If I could perpetually live in that one year on a loop I would!

Thank you to the University of Hartford Jackie McLean Fellowship and the History Department. I also owe a debt of gratitude to City College of New York's Center for Worker Education, to Kathlene McDonald for her support of my professional development, and to librarian Seamus Scanlon for renewing books that were well beyond the limit.

Curators Ida E. Jones and JoEllen El Bashir and library technician Richard Jenkins at Howard University's Moorland-Spingarn Research Center made my archival trips and research requests both fruitful and painless. Thank you, Professor Jones, for championing my work and Mrs. El Bashir for fielding my last-minute requests. Sara Winter has also been a mentor over the years, translating for me and putting into perspective milestones and setbacks alike.

In the last four years, work on the completion of this book was made possible through California State University–Sacramento grants, including the College of Arts and Letters Research, Scholarly and Creative Activity funding, the university's Research and Creative Activity Faculty Award, the Retirees' Association Faculty Development Fund, and the Probationary Faculty Award. I've benefited from the comments and critiques of colleagues Tristan Josephson, Mark Ocegueda, Christopher Towler, and Mark Brown during our participation in the Faculty Scholarship Community "Race, Ethnicity, Identities, and Global Bodies in Motion." I also appreciate the support of my dean, Sheree Meyer, my chairs, Aaron Cohen and Jeffrey Wilson, Rebecca Kluchin, and other members of the CSUS History Department. I have also had the pleasure and privilege of working with so many amazing students at Sacramento State, who, through their questions, comments, conversations, and close readings, helped me engage more deeply in the theoretical and methodological framing for this project. These include Antoine Johnson, Vanessa Madrigal Lauchland, and the spring 2019 graduate reading seminar in US historiography.

My service to CSUS also brought people into my orbit, or I was brought into theirs. Either way, these are folks without whose fellowship and commiseration this project could not have seen completion. They helped me build community in Sacramento, made space for my full self, and they have my deepest gratitude. Joshua and Topaz Wiscons, Lynn Tashiro, John Johnson, Todd Migliaccio, Diana Tate Vermeire, Christopher Kent, Tristan Josephson, Jessie Gaston, and Saray Ayala Lopez were always people I was happy to see. A special shout out goes to Dana Kivel, who introduced me to spinning. Thank you for including me in supper club before you even really knew me, for errand trips, and for the generosity of your listening ear. I deeply value your comradeship.

I've met so many influential folks at and through conferences and symposia over the last few years who have reaffirmed and confirmed the work in this book when they uttered the word "interiority" or when they made a comment, asked a question, or shared advice: LaKisha Simmons, Craig Steven Wilder, Brian Purnell, Laura Helton, Lindsey Jones, Aisha Finch, K. T. Ewing, Fath Davis Ruffins, Penny Von Eschen, Robyn Spencer, Krystal Appiah, and reader number 2 as yet unknown. One person, though, stands out and subsequently deserves any praise that may come for this book. I met Corinne T. Field when she chaired an ASALH (Association for the Study of African American Life and History) panel in fall 2015. Despite the fact that my luggage did not show up, and I wore sneakers to my session, Cori engaged seriously with my research. Since then, Cori has supported this book's publication, providing the most generous, detailed, and genius feedback and suggestions, and fielding all of my questions. I deeply hope this book lives up to her standards of what it could be! Thank you also to Shana Agid and Thomas Hafer for their eyes on the near-final product. And thank you to Production Director Martin Coleman and copy editor John Raymond whose engagement with the manuscript made so much difference.

It's important to have a woman of color cypher: longtime sista-friend Armisey Smith has been a mainstay, as have Jessica Krug, Karen Tejada Pena, Amaka Okechukwu, Kelly Elaine Navies, Devyn Spence Benson, Nicole Burrowes, Chris Kelsaw, Deirdre Cooper Owens, Ujju Aggarwal, Laura Liu, and the literal whole Association of Black Women Historians! Rachel Herzing deserves a special mention: after my move from New York, she adopted me and hosted me for regular pork belly hash brunches, day drinking, and distillery trips, and she (and Isaac Ontiveros) included me in Center for Political Education events that helped me settle into my Northern California life. In true Golden Girls fashion, thank you for being my friends.

Dear friends, chosen, biological, and animal family, and systems of self-care are important factors in what makes a successful scholar (and person). Shana Agid, Jill Magi, Kerry Ann MacNeil, Betsy Thorleifson, Jey Born, Jonny Farrow, Armisey Smith, Shelley Austin, and Patricia Saheed believe in and love me. Shana and Jill have both not only shared with me the kind of meditations on my work and the world that only artist-theoreticians can, they have both reflected back to me a vision of myself that I hoped was true, but that I could not always see as I reckoned with grief, imposter syndrome, feelings of shame, and fears of failure. They imagined a future for me that I could not see, and they still do. Along with Lauren Santangelo, Logan McBride, and Thomas Hafer, they reminded me to (literally) keep swimming, to go to the chiropractor, and to see the acupuncturist. I am deeply grateful for the work, the sometimes actual physical labor, my chosen kin have all done in keeping me afloat, fed, clothed in clean laundry, and in the world. (Thanks to Anne Hamel and Susan Fleming for their professional services as well.) Finally, many of my machinations and decisions in life have been made to hold space for Nasia Shlasinger. My relationship with her, and with her brothers Ari and Jordan early on, created in me a deep understanding of and appreciation for the intellectual capacities of young people. Lastly, Mocca the cat provided the kind of unconditional love, companionship, and attention one must have to thrive. I still miss you, Moke!

NOTES

INTRODUCTION

1 Hicks, *Talk with You Like a Woman*, 1–5.

2 See Wilma King's discussion about the difficulty of using Works Progress Administration (WPA) narratives, not merely because of the age of subjects but also because of the power differential experienced by subjects in the interview process, "Remembering the Emancipation," *African American Childhoods*, 74.

3 Two examples that illuminate the class and cultural distinctions between a mostly northern urban black intelligentsia and poor and working-class black masses are Sterling Stuckey's *Slave Culture: Nationalist Theory and the Foundations of Black America* (New York: Oxford University Press, 1987) and Wilson Jeremiah Moses's *The Wings of Ethiopia: Studies in African-American Life and Letters* (Ames: Iowa State University Press, 1990).

4 Johnson, "On Agency," 121.

5 Curwood, *Stormy Weather*, 7; Quashie, *Sovereignty of Quiet*.

6 Influenced by both a social and cultural turn brought about by the rights revolutions of the late 1960s and 1970s and by racial unrest in urban centers, scholarship about interwar and post–World War II migration identified a "ghetto synthesis model," manifesting in works like Gilbert Osofky's *Harlem: The Making of a Ghetto, 1890–1930* (New York: Harper and Row, 1966) and Allan Spear's *Black Chicago: The Making of a Negro Ghetto, 1890–1920* (Chicago: University of Chicago Press, 1967). This material focused on the development of an "underclass," partly as a result of black migration. See Gunnar Myrdal's use of the term in his *The Challenge to Affluence* [New York: Pantheon Books, 1963], and Michael B. Katz, "The Urban 'Underclass' as a Metaphor of Social Transformation," in *The "Underclass" Debate: Views from History*, ed. Michael B. Katz [Princeton, NJ: Princeton University Press, 1993], 3–23. By the 1970s, the term was used by journalists, and by the 1980s—as the aftermath of fiscal crises and fiscal austerity responses took hold, increasing the number of poor people without access to social services in cities—the term "underclass" referred to an inner-city pathology: long-term welfare recipients, high school dropouts, drug addicts, street criminals and hustlers, and a growing population of the homeless unemployed and the homeless mentally ill. Other publications in the ghetto synthesis tradition include David Katzman, *Before the Ghetto: Black Detroit in the Nineteenth Century* (Urbana: University of Illinois Press, 1973); Kenneth L. Kusmer, *A Ghetto Takes Shape: Black Cleveland, 1870–1930* (Urbana: University of Illinois Press, 1976);

Thomas Philpott, *The Slum and the Ghetto* (New York: Oxford University Press, 1978). See Joe W. Trotter, "African Americans in the City: The Industrial Era, 1900–1950," in *The New African American Urban History*, ed. Kenneth W. Goings and Raymond A. Mohl (Thousand Oaks, CA: Sage Publications, 1996), 308, and Borchert, *Alley Life in Washington.*

7   "Johnson," Frazier Papers, Box 131–113, Folder 15.

8   Carolyn Steedman, "Culture, Cultural Studies and the Historians," in *The Cultural Studies Readers*, ed. Simon During (New York: Routledge, 1993), 50.

9   Christopher Castiglia, "Interiority," in *Keywords for American Cultural Studies*, ed. Bruce Burgett and Glenn Hendler (New York: New York University Press, 2007), 135–137; Lindsey, "Configuring Modernities," 7, and Lindsey, *Colored No More*, 56.

10 Tina Campt, *Listening to Images* (Durham, NC: Duke University Press, 2017), 8; Quashie, *Sovereignty of Quiet*, 23–24.

11 Quashie, *Sovereignty of Quiet*, 6.

12 Campt, *Listening to Images*, 10.

13 Borchert, *Alley Life in Washington*, ix–x; Joe William Trotter Jr. provides a comprehensive examination of the relationship between migration and the "ghetto model of black urban history" in his literature review that appears in *The Great Migration in Historical Perspective*, 1–21.

14 Federal Writers' Project, Works Progress Administration, *Washington City and Capital* (Washington, DC: U.S. Government Printing Office, 1937), 88; *WPA Guide to Washington, D.C.*, 51–59.

15 Histories on black DC that have mostly adhered to highlighting black achievements include Dyson, *Howard University*; Dabney, *History of Schools for Negroes*; Green, *Secret City*; Michael R. Winston, *The Howard University Department of History: 1913–1973* (Washington, DC: Howard University, 1973); Cantwell, "Anacostia"; Alfred A. Moss, *The American Negro Academy: The Voice of the Talented Tenth* (Baton Rouge: Louisiana State University Press, 1981); Nina Honemond Clarke, *History of the Nineteenth-Century Black Churches in Maryland and Washington, D.C.* (New York: Vantage Press, 1983); Michael Fitzpatrick, "'A Great Agitation for Business': Black Economic Development in Shaw," *Washington History* 2 (Fall–Winter 1990–91): 48–73; Lois E. Horton, "The Days of Jubilee: Black Migration during the Civil War and Reconstruction," Spencer Crew, "Melding the Old and the New: The Modern African American Community, 1930–1960," and Keith Q. Warner, "From 'Down the Way Where the Nights Are Gay': Caribbean Immigrants and the Bridging of Cultures," all in *Urban Odyssey: A Multicultural History of Washington, D.C.*, ed. Francine Curro Cary (Washington, DC: Smithsonian Institution Press, 1996); Moore, *Leading the Race*; McQuirter, "Claiming the City"; Miller, "Black Washington and the New Negro"; Stewart, *First Class.*

16 Moore, *Leading the Race*, 2–3.

17 Miller, "Where Is the Negro's Heaven?," 425–426.

18 Jessica Ellen Sewell defines these landscapes in the following way: "imagined," how the built landscape is "conceived of and understood by individuals within a group," specifically "culturally dominant imaginings" and the "experienced landscape," how "actual people used [the built landscape] in daily practice, [which] is highly dependent on the social position of the person experiencing it." Sewell, *Women and the Everyday City*, xiv–xxi.

19 Gillette, *Between Justice and Beauty*, x–xii. The language of "neglected neighbors" comes from social reformer Charles Weller's turn of the twentieth century study of DC's impoverished communities, *Neglected Neighbors*.

20 Lipsitz, "Racialization of Space and the Spatialization of Race," 17.

21 Borchert, *Alley Life in Washington*, 218–219.

22 Clark-Lewis, *Living In, Living Out*.

23 Clark-Lewis, *Living In, Living Out*, 6.

24 The most well-known and influential of these works include St. Clair Drake and Horace Cayton, *Black Metropolis: A Study of Negro Life in a Northern City* (Chicago: University of Chicago Press, 1945); Allan Spear, *Black Chicago: The Making of a Negro Ghetto, 1890–1920* (Chicago: University of Chicago Press, 1967); Robert C. Weaver, *The Negro Ghetto* (New York: Harcourt, Brace and Company, 1948); Kenneth Clark, *Dark Ghetto: Dilemmas of Social Power* (New York: Harper and Row, 1965); August Meier and Elliot Rudwick, *From Plantation to Ghetto* (New York, Hill and Wang, 1966).

25 Craig Steven Wilder's commentary for American Historical Association panel, "When the Ghetto Is Not Enough, or in Some Cases Too Much: New African American Urban Identities for the Great Migration and Beyond," January 2014, Washington, DC.

26 Bay et al., *Intellectual History of Black Women*, 4.

27 Editor Ben Highmore's introduction to George Perec's "Approaches to What?" (1973) in *Everyday Life Reader* (New York: Routledge, 2002), 176. I'm also grateful to Herman Bennett and his 2019 presentation at the African American Intellectual History Society meeting at the University of Michigan, Ann Arbor.

28 Wilson, "'This Past Was Waiting for Me When I Came,'" 346, 354; Michele Mitchell, "Turns of the Kaleidoscope: 'Race,' Ethnicity, and Analytical Patterns in American Women's Gender History," *Journal of Women's History* 25, no. 4 (2013): 46–73, 46; see also Brewer, "Theorizing Race, Class and Gender."

29 Favor, *Authentic Blackness*; Judith Butler, *Gender Trouble: Feminism and the Subversion of Identity* (New York: Routledge, 1990).

30 Curwood, *Stormy Weather*, 7.

31 The following are a few who have informed my methodological practice. These have changed the shape of women's/gender history and the history of women of African descent by both engaging and reconfiguring race and feminist theory: bell hooks, *Ain't I a Woman: Black Women and Feminism* (Boston: South End Press, 1981); Paula Giddings, *When and Where I Enter: The Impact of Black*

Women on Race and Sex in America (New York: William Morrow, 1984); Deborah Gray White, *Ar'n't I a Woman: Female Slaves in the Plantation South* (New York: W. W. Norton, 1985); Joan Scott, "Gender: A Useful Category of Historical Analysis," *American Historical Review* 91 (December 1986); Hortense J. Spillers, "Mama's Baby, Papa's Maybe: An American Grammar Book," *Diacritics* 17, no. 2 (Summer 1987): 64–81; Hazel V. Carby, *Reconstructing Womanhood: The Emergence of the Afro-American Woman Novelist* (New York: Oxford University Press, 1987); Elsa Barkley Brown, "'What Has Happened Here': The Politics of Difference in Women's History and Feminist Politics," *Feminist Studies* 18 (Summer 1992): 295–312; Higginbotham, "African American Women's History and the Metalanguage of Race"; Darlene Clark Hine, *Hine Sight: Black Women and the Re-Construction of American History* (Bloomington: Indiana University Press, 1994); Michele Mitchell, "Silences Broken, Silences Kept: Gender and Sexuality in African American History," *Gender and History* 11, no. 3 (November 1999): 433–444; Jennifer L. Morgan, *Laboring Women: Reproduction and Gender in New World Slavery* (Philadelphia: University of Pennsylvania Press, 2004); Hartman, "Venus in Two Acts," 11. See also Hunter, *To 'Joy Their Freedom*; Harley, "When Your Work Is Not Who You Are"; "Gender Roles in Black Communities, 1880s–1930," by Sharon Harley, http://www.wilsoncenter.org/sites/default/files/harley.pdf; Rayford W. Logan, *The Negro in American Life and Thought: The Nadir, 1877–1901* (New York: Dial Press, 1954).

32 Hartman, "Venus in Two Acts," 11.

33 See, for example, Kathy Peiss, *Cheap Amusements: Working Class Women and Leisure in Turn of the Century New York* (Philadelphia: Temple University Press, 1986); David Nasaw, *Going Out: The Rise and Fall of Public Amusements* (Cambridge, MA: Harvard University Press, 1999); Roy Rosenzweig, *Eight Hours for What We Will: Workers and Leisure in an Industrial City, 1870–1921* (Cambridge: Cambridge University Press, 1983).

34 Harley, "When Your Work Is Not Who You Are."

35 See Kyra Gaunt, *The Games Black Girls Play: Learning the Ropes from Double Dutch to Hip Hop* (New York: New York University Press, 2006); Ruth Nicole Brown, *Black Girlhood Celebration: Toward a Hip-Hop Feminist Pedagogy* (New York: Peter Lang, 2009); Maisha Winn, *Girl Time: Literacy, Justice, and the School to Prison Pipeline* (New York: Teachers College Press, 2011); Brown, *Hear Our Truths*; Cox, *Shapeshifters*; Chatelain, *South Side Girls*; Simmons, *Crescent City Girls*; Field et al., "History of Black Girlhood"; see also early works, including Joyce A. Ladner, *Tomorrow's Tomorrow: The Black Woman* (Garden City, NY: Doubleday, 1971); Rebecca Carroll, *Sugar in the Raw: Voices of Young Black Girls in America* (New York: Three Rivers Press, 1997).

36 King, *Stolen Childhood*, xviii; Marie Jenkins Schwartz, *Born in Bondage: Growing Up Enslaved in the Antebellum South* (Cambridge, MA: Harvard University Press, 2000).

37 King, *African American Childhoods*, 5.

38 Mintz, *Huck's Raft*, 2.

39 Mintz, *Huck's Raft*, 2–4; Hawes, *Children between the Wars*, 13. In addition, see the following for not only a discussion of the history of children but also the evolving nature of the concept of childhood, specifically in the early twentieth century during which "child science" was in development in the field of psychology: *American Childhood: A Research Guide and Historical Handbook*, ed. Joseph H. Hawes and N. Ray Hiner (Westport, CT: Greenwood Press, 1985); Lindenmeyer, *Greatest Generation Grows Up*; Wolcott, *Cops and Kids*.

40 Bernstein, *Racial Innocence*, 233, 198.

41 Chatelain, *South Side Girls*, 5, 6, 14.

42 Frazier, *Negro Youth at the Crossways*.

43 Chatelain, *South Side Girls*, 6.

44 Chatelain, "'Most Interesting Girl in This Country Is the Colored Girl,'" 6; see also Aimee Meredith Cox's discussion on the uses of the "thick descriptions" of ethnography in *Shapeshifters*, viii.

45 Johnson, *Growing Up in the Black Belt*.

46 Cahn, *Sexual Reckonings*.

47 Hartman, *Wayward Lives, Beautiful Experiments*, xiv–xv.

48 Darlene Clark Hine, "Rape and the Inner Lives of Black Women in the Middle West," *Signs: Journal of Women in Culture and Society* 14, no. 4 (1989): 915.

49 Cahn, *Sexual Reckonings*, 102.

50 Hartman, *Wayward Lives, Beautiful Experiments*, 348.

51 Mitchell, *Righteous Propagation*, 171; Gaines, *Uplifting the Race*, 177.

52 Hicks, *Talk with You Like a Woman*, 4, 1–5.

53 Jones, *Recreation and Amusement* and *Housing of Negroes in Washington, D.C.*; Frazier, *Negro Family in the United States* and *Negro Youth at the Crossways*.

54 Dewhirst, "Recreational Opportunities for the Adolescent Girl in Washington, D.C."; Johnson, "Transformation of Juvenile Gangs into Accommodated Groups"; Mason, "Study of the Supervision of Twenty-Five Parolees"; Mugrauer, "Cultural Study of Ten Negro Girls in an Alley"; Ober, "Social Hygiene Society of Washington, D.C."; Ratigan, "Sociological Survey of Disease in Four Alleys"; Sellew, "Deviant Social Situation"; Somerville, "Study of a Group of Negro Children Living in an Alley Culture."

55 Frazier, *Negro Youth at the Crossways*.

56 Frazier, *Negro Youth at the Crossways*, xxxv, n4.

57 Frazier, *Negro Youth at the Crossways*, xxxv, n4.

58 Frazier, *Negro Youth at the Crossways*, xxxv, n4.

59 Letter from Frazier to Mrs. Margaret Hunton, interviewer on the Harlem study, August 11, 1938, Frazier Papers Box 131–40, Folder 10, MSRC.

60 Robert Gregg, "Giant Steps: W.E.B. Du Bois and the Historical Enterprise," in *W.E.B. Du Bois, Race and the City: The Philadelphia Negro and Its Legacy*, ed.

Michael B. Katz and Thomas J. Sugrue (Philadelphia: University of Pennsylvania Press, 1988), 83–85; Du Bois, *Philadelphia Negro*, 311.

61 See Darlene Clark Hine, "Rape and the Inner Lives of Black Women in the Middle West," *Signs* 14, no. 4 (1989): 915.

62 LaKisha Simmons defines this as "relationships of power expressed through spatial economies." See Simmons, *Crescent City Girls*, 13.

63 Du Bois, *Souls of Black Folks*, xi.

64 Here I am rather rudimentarily referring to the "rights" that form the basis of David Harvey's call for a reclaiming of these rights in his "The Right to the City," where he defines them as not only "the individual liberty to access urban resources" but also "the right to change ourselves by changing the city," "a common right [. . .] to reshape the processes of urbanization," "the freedom to make and remake our cities and ourselves," and "the most precious yet most neglected of our human rights." Harvey, "The Right to the City," 1. I am also employing David Delany's notion that Jim Crow's system of racial segregation as a "legal landscape" produces experiences of "rights" and "obligations" related to location: Delany, *Race, Place, and the Law 1836–1948*, 14.

CHAPTER 1. "A CHRONIC PATIENT FOR THE SOCIOLOGICAL CLINIC"

1 Chapter title from Locke, "Enter the New Negro," 632.

2 Du Bois, *Dusk of Dawn*, 58–59.

3 Baker, *From Savage to Negro*, 176–177.

4 Holloway, *Confronting the Veil*; see also St. Clair Drake's introduction to the 1967 edition of Frazier's *Negro Youth at the Crossways*, v–xx.

5 Jarmon, "E. Franklin Frazier's Sociology of Race and Class," 90–91; Frazier, "Pathology of Race Prejudice," 855–866.

6 Du Bois, *Dusk of Dawn*, 58; Morris, "Sociology of Race and W.E.B Du Bois and the Path Not Taken," 504–506.

7 See Du Bois's chapters in *Dusk of Dawn*, "Science and Empire" and "The Concept of Race."

8 Williams, *From Caste to a Minority*; Du Bois, *Philadelphia Negro*; Charles Camic, "On the Edge: Sociology during the Great Depression and the New Deal," in *Sociology in America: A History*, ed. Craig Calhoun (Chicago: University of Chicago Press, 2007), 230–233.

9 Du Bois, *Philadelphia Negro*.

10 Moynihan, *Negro Family*.

11 Robert L. Sutherland, "Report of Progress on the Negro Youth Study of the American Youth Commission," n.d., Frazier Papers, Box 131–25, Folder 5.

12 Sutherland, *Color, Class and Personality*, xiv–xv; see also Howard Winant, "The Dark Side of the Force: One Hundred Years of the Sociology of Race," in *Sociology in America: A History*, ed. Craig Calhoun (Chicago: University of Chicago Press, 2007), 550–553.

13 Myrdal, *American Dilemma*.
14 Frazier, *Negro Youth*, 261.
15 Reid, *In a Minor Key*; Davis and Dollard, *Children of Bondage*; Warner, *Color and Human Nature*; Johnson, *Growing Up in the Black Belt*.
16 Frazier, *Negro Youth*, 290.
17 Frazier, *Negro Youth*, 261.
18 Frazier, *Negro Youth*, 39, 40.
19 Frazier, *Negro Youth*, 261.
20 Hawes, *Children between the Wars*, 1–32.
21 Hawes, *Children between the Wars*, 1–12, 51–85.
22 Wolcott, *Cops and Kids*, 196–197.
23 Locke, "Enter the New Negro," 632.
24 Locke, *New Negro*, 9.
25 Locke, "Enter the New Negro," 632, 634.
26 Locke, "Enter the New Negro," 632; Baker, *From Savage to Negro*, 150–152.
27 Sitkoff, *New Deal for Blacks*; Harlan E. Glazier, "No Negro Need Apply: A Brief Glance at Employment Situation in the District of Columbia as Related to Colored Citizens" pamphlet, n.d., Printed Material, Box C-435, NAACP Paper Manuscript Division, Library of Congress; Pacifico, "Don't Buy Where You Can't Work"; Green, *Secret City*, 223–224, 228; Sullivan, *Days of Hope*; Cohen, *Making a New Deal*; Asch and Musgrove, *Chocolate City*, 250–251; *Federal Writer's Project WPA Guide*, 506.
28 Jones, *Recreation and Amusement*, xi.
29 Jones, *Recreation and Amusement*, 161.
30 Jones, *Recreation and Amusement*, 193–194.
31 Jones, *Housing of Negroes in Washington, D.C.*, 69.
32 Jones, *Housing of Negroes*, 69.
33 Asch and Musgrove, *Chocolate City*, 238.
34 Charles Camic, "On the Edge: Sociology during the Great Depression and the New Deal," in *Sociology in America: A History*, ed. Craig Calhoun (Chicago: University of Chicago Press, 2007), 230; Baker, *From Savage to Negro*, 177–178.
35 Howard Winant, "The Dark Side of the Force: One Hundred Years of the Sociology of Race," in *Sociology in America: A History*, ed. Craig Calhoun (Chicago: University of Chicago Press, 2007), 553.
36 Jones, *Recreation and Amusement*, 21, 25.
37 Jones, *Housing of Negroes*, 152–153.
38 Baker, *From Savage to Negro*, 176–178.
39 Jones, *Recreation and Amusement*, xii; Jones, *Housing of Negroes*.
40 James Farr, "Political Science," in *Cambridge History of Science*, ed. Porter and Ross, 315, 316–319.
41 Emphasis added. Quoted in Dorothy Ross, "Changing Contours of the Social Science Disciplines," in *Cambridge History of Science*, ed. Porter and Ross, 227.

42 Hawes, *Children between the Wars*, 70–85.

43 Reid, *In a Minor Key*, foreword by Floyd W. Reeves, director of the Commission, preface by associate director Robert Sutherland, 112; Robert L. Sutherland, "Report of Progress on the Negro Youth Study of the American Youth Commission," Frazier Papers, Box 131–25, Folder 5; Sutherland, *Color, Class, and Personality*, xxiii, 79, 96, 110.

44 Helen Swick Perry, introduction to Sullivan, *Fusion of Psychiatry and Social Science*, xvii; Johnson shared the cost of Harry Stuck Sullivan with Frazier to produce Johnson's research "on analysis of personality documents concerning Negro youth" in the South. See letter from Johnson to Frazier, January 20, 1939, Frazier Papers, Box 131–25, Folder 4.

45 Charles S. Johnson, "Harry Stack Sullivan, Social Scientist," in The *Fusion of Psychiatry and Social Science* (New York: W. W. Norton, 1964), xxxiv; Johnson, "The Contributions of Harry Stack Sullivan to Sociology," in *The Contributions of Harry Stack Sullivan: A Symposium on Interpersonal Theory in Psychiatry and Social Science*, ed. Patrick Mullahy (New York: Science House, 1967), 209–210.

46 Baker, *From Savage to Negro*, 175.

47 Baker, *From Savage to Negro*, 172.

48 Ratigan cited contemporary and local studies about the relationship between rates of disease and socioeconomic status in her chapter "Repudiation of the Racial Theories of Disease" in her dissertation "A Sociological Survey of Disease in Four Alleys in the National Capital."

49 Ratigan, "Sociological Survey of Disease in Four Alleys."

50 Sellew, "Deviant Social Situation," vii, 16.

51 Sellew, "Deviant Social Situation," 16.

52 Sellew, "Deviant Social Situation," 42.

53 Muhammad, *Condemnation of Blackness*, 9; Baker, *From Savage to Negro*, chapter 5, "Rethinking Race at the Turn of the Century," discusses Du Bois and Boas and their roles in shifting this discourse in an effort to "assert racial equality" in opposition to both social Darwinism and eugenics of the previous decades.

54 "Biographical Note," Guide to Allison Davis Papers 1932–1984, University of Chicago Library. https://www.lib.uchicago.edu.

55 O'Connor, *Poverty Knowledge*, 65.

56 Frazier, *Negro Family in the United States*, 180–181.

57 Frazier, *Negro Family in the United States*, 205.

58 Frazier, *Negro Family in the United States*, 354–357.

59 Frazier, *Negro Family in the United States*, 348–349.

60 Frazier, *Negro Family in the United States*, 108–9, 343, 352.

61 Frazier, *Negro Family in the United States*, 353.

62 Frazier, *Negro Family in the United States*, 288–290.

63 Frazier, *Negro Family in the United States*, 356–357.

64 August Meier and Elliot Rudwick, *From Plantation to Ghetto* (New York: Hill and Wang, 1976); Trotter, *Black Milwaukee*.

65 Sullivan, "Chapter IX: A Psychiatric Gloss," 7, Frazier Papers, Box 131 – 41, folder 15. This chapter also appears as chapter VIII in *Negro Youth at the Crossways*, a case study on "Warren Wall," which was the pseudonym for Myron Ross Jr. See Frazier, *Negro Youth at the Crossways*, 231.

66 Sullivan, "Chapter IX: A Psychiatric Gloss," 5, Frazier Papers, Box 131 – 41, folder 15. This chapter also appears as chapter VIII in *Negro Youth at the Crossways*, a case study on "Warren Wall," which was the pseudonym for Myron Ross Jr. See Frazier, *Negro Youth at the Crossways*, 231.

67 Frazier, *Negro Youth at the Crossways*, 263–264.

68 Ratigan, "Sociological Survey of Disease in Four Alleys," xii.

69 Sellew, "Deviant Social Situation," 16.

70 Somerville, "Study of a Group of Negro Children Living in an Alley Culture," 1–2, 9.

71 Carby, "Policing the Black Woman's Body in an Urban Context," 739–740.

72 Frazier, *Negro Youth at the Crossways*, 261, 290.

73 "R. G. Bernreuter, 93, Psychology Teacher," *New York Times*, June 20, 1995.

74 Laura Lee and Dennis Nelson were identified as "interviewers," while Ruth Bittler and Thomas Davis were "research workers." Frazier, *Negro Youth at the Crossways*, 295; Letter from Frazier to Dr. Robert L. Sutherland, February 10, 1938, Frazier Papers, Box 131–41, Folder 2.

75 Letter from Frazier to Dr. Robert L. Sutherland, February 17, 1938, Frazier Papers, Box 131–41, Folder 2; 1940 United States Census, 1930 United States Census s.v. "Thomas Edward Davis," Washington, DC, accessed through Ancestry.com.

76 Letter from Frances Williams of the YWCA to E. Franklin Frazier, February 24, 1938; Letter from Frazier to Frances Williams, March 3, 1938, Frazier Papers, Box 131–33, Folder 29.

77 1940 United States Census, s.v. "Laura Lee," Washington, DC, accessed through Ancestry.com.

78 Susie Morgan, WDC 22, Frazier Papers, Box 131–112, Folder 11; Box 131–113, Folder 13.

79 Dennis D. Nelson, "Application for Position," to National Youth Study, American Youth Commission of the U.S. Department of Labor, March 18, 1938; Letter from Dennis D. Nelson to E. Franklin Frazier, March 7, 1938; Letter from Herbert Bigelow to E. Franklin Frazier, March 17, 1938, Frazier Papers, Box 131–33, Folder 29.

80 Letter from Ira De A. Reid to E. Franklin Frazier, May 2, 1938; Letter from Jean Westmoreland to E. Franklin Frazier, June 14, 1938, Frazier Papers, Box 131–34, Folder 2; 1930 United States Census, s.v. "Jean P. Westmoreland."

81 Letter from E. Franklin Frazier to Robert L. Sutherland, July 13, 1938, Frazier Papers, Box 131–41, Folder 7; 1940 United States Census, s.v. "Isadore Miles."

82 "Staff Selection," Frazier Papers, Box 131–141, Folder 17; 1940 United States Census, s.v. "Ruth J. Bittler."

83 1940 United States Census, s.v. "Zulme S. MacNeal"; Frazier, *Negro Youth at the Crossways*, 295.

84 Baker, *From Savage to Negro*, 125–126.

85 Carby, "Policing the Black Woman's Body in an Urban Context," 740–741; see also Khalil Muhammad's introduction, "The Mismeasure of Crime," in *The Condemnation of Blackness*, 1–14.

86 Sullivan, "Chapter IX: A Psychiatric Gloss," 2, in *The Fusion of Psychiatry and Social Science*.

CHAPTER 2. "COURSE WE KNOW WE AIN'T GOT NO BUSINESS THERE, BUT THAT'S WHY WE GO IN"

1 "Southwest Community," Ruth J. Bittler, Frazier Papers, Frazier Papers, Box 131–41, Folder 8.

2 Williams, *Images of America*; Gillette, part 3, "The City and the Modern State," in *Between Justice and Beauty*, 135–207; Keith Melder, "Southwest Washington: Where History Stopped," in *Washington at Home*, ed. Smith, 89–105; Groves, " Development of a Black Residential Community in Southwest Washington," 270–272.

3 Asch and Musgrove, *Chocolate City*, 196–210, 227, 251, 273.

4 Groves, "Development of a Black Residential Community in Southwest Washington," 270–272; "Re: Fourth Street Southwest," May 9, 1938, Box 131–112, Folder 7, NYS-DC, Research Projects; Susie Morgan, Frazier Papers, Box 131–112, Folder 11; Box 131–113, Folder 13.

5 Asch and Musgrove, *Chocolate City*, 201.

6 *WPA Guide to Washington, D.C.*, 112.

7 Abbott, *Political Terrain*, 104.

8 Weller, *Neglected Neighbors*, 71–73.

9 Gillette, *Between Justice and Beauty*, 112–113.

10 Quoted in Gillette, *Between Justice and Beauty*, 116.

11 Gillette, *Between Justice and Beauty*, 115–117; Jacob Riis, "Some Things We Drink," *New York Evening Sun*, August 21, 1891; Riis, *How the Other Half Lives*.

12 Quoted in Gillette, *Between Justice and Beauty*, 113.

13 Gillette, *Between Justice and Beauty*, 113–114.

14 See chapter 1 in James Borchert, "The Rise and Fall of Washington's Inhabited Alleys," in *Alley Life in Washington*; Jones, *Directory of Inhabited Alleys of Washington, D.C.*; Jones, *Housing of Negroes in Washington, D.C.*, 41–51, 47–48.

15 Gillette, *Between Justice and Beauty*, 119; *Washington Star*, December 27, 1908; May 6, 20, 30, 1907 (editorials).

16 Asch and Musgrove, *Chocolate City*, 208.

17 Quoted in Baker, *Following the Color Line*, 113.

18 Wilkerson, *Warmth of Other Suns*, 200.

19 Elizabeth Clark-Lewis, "'For a Real Better Life': Voices of African American Women Migrants, 1900–1930," in *Urban Odyssey*, ed. Cary, 99.

20 Asch and Musgrove, *Chocolate City*, 196–210, 227, 251, 273.

21 Mitchell, *Cultural Geography*, 100.

22 See Asch and Musgrove, "National Show Town" and "There Is a New Negro to Be Reckoned With," in *Chocolate City*.

23 Landis, *Segregation in Washington*, 22–23, 44–45, 88.

24 Sewell, *Women and the Everyday City*, xiv–xxi; Delany, *Race, Place, and the Law*, 4, 5, 6–14.

25 See chapter 1 for more on Howard University; also see Asch and Musgrove, *Chocolate City*, 168–173.

26 Dyson, *Howard University*.

27 Terrell, *Colored Woman in a White World*, 383–384.

28 For more on the response to the restricted movements of black middle-class and elite Washingtonians, see *Picturing the Promise*, ed. Gardullo et al., 120–155; Du Bois, "The Secret City," 185–187; Holloway, *Confronting the Veil*, 35–43; Spencer Crew, "Melding the Old and the New," in *Urban Odyssey: A Multicultural History of Washington, D.C.*, ed. Francine Curro Cury (Washington, DC: Smithsonian Institution Press, 1996), 220; for the development and achievements of DC's black middle and aspiring class, see Moore, *Leading the Race*.

29 Asch and Musgrove, *Chocolate City*, 243–248.

30 McKittrick, *Demonic Grounds*, xiv.

31 David Harvey defines Henri Lefebvre's "right to the city" as "a right to change ourselves by changing the city. [. . .] a common rather than an individual right since this transformation inevitably depends upon the exercise of a collective power to reshape the processes of urbanization." See Harvey's "Right to the City," 23. Lefebvre identifies the "right to the city" as a "cry and a demand," "a right to urban life." See Henri Lefebvre, *Writings on Cities*, trans. and ed. Eleonore Kofman and Elizabeth Lebas (Malden, MA: Blackwell Publishers, 1996), 39–46.

32 Frazier, *Negro Youth*, xxvii–xxxiii; James Richmond, Frazier Papers, Box 131–111, Folder 8.

33 Frazier, *Negro Youth*, xxvii, xxx.

34 Frazier, *Negro Youth*, xvii–xxx.

35 James Richmond, Frazier Papers, Box 131–111, Folder 8.

36 Frazier, *Negro Youth*, xxx.

37 Frazier, *Negro Youth*, xxx–xxxi.

38 James Richmond, Frazier Papers, Box 131–111, Folder 8; Frazier, *Negro Youth*, xxviii, xxx.

39 WDC XXVII (Ellsworth Davis), Frazier Papers, Box 131–74, Folders 3–10 (notecards); Box 131–111, Folders 3–5 (notecards); Box 131–112, Folder 6 (notecards); 1940 United States Census, s.v. "Ellsworth Davis."

40 Susie Morgan interviewed with Frazier's staff person Laura Lee for over a year and possibly longer, as Lee documented that she and her mother had begun to spend time with Susie outside of the research relationship and that Lee had begun to feel that the interviews were exploitative and noted that she would rather befriend Susie to see if she could help her change some of the circumstances of her life. "Susie WDC 22," Frazier Papers, Box 131–112, Folder 11, 12; Box 131–113, Folder 13.

41 1920 United States Census, s.v. "Susie Morgan."

42 Weller, *Neglected Neighbors*; Jones, *Directory of Inhabited Alleys of Washington, D.C.*

43 This description is provided by E. Franklin Frazier's staff interviewer, Laura Lee, who was assigned to "lower class girls," which included Susie Morgan.

44 "Re: Fourth Street Southwest," May 9, 1938, Box 131–112, Folder 7, NYS-DC, Research Projects, EFFP.

45 See chapter 1 in James Borchert, "The Rise and Fall of Washington's Inhabited Alleys," in *Alley Life in Washington*; D.C. Historic Preservation Alley Survey, https://planning.dc.gov, 8; see also the amendment to the DC Alley Dwelling Act 1944, Library of Congress, https://www.loc.gov.

46 Gillette, *Between Justice and Beauty*, 142.

47 John Ildher, director of the ADA, wrote in his diary of the conditions he found in alley houses on visits with E. Franklin Frazier; see Gillette, *Between Justice and Beauty*, 143–144.

48 Susie Morgan, WDC 22, Frazier Papers, Box 131–112, Folder 11; Box 131–113, Folder 13.

49 Susie Morgan, WDC 22, Frazier Papers, Box 131–112, Folder 11; Box 131–113, Folder 13; "Development of the Central Area West and East of the Capitol—Washington D.C. 1941," map available through Library of Congress, http://www.loc.gov.

50 Susie Morgan, WDC 22, Frazier Papers, Box 131–112, Folder 11; Box 131–113, Folder 13.

51 Lewis, *District of Columbia*, 75; Asch and Musgrove, *Chocolate City*, 237–238. There is some disagreement about whether Moton was seated in the segregated section. See Scott A. Sandage, "A Marble House Divided: The Lincoln Memorial, the Civil Rights Movement, and the Politics of Memory, 1939–1963," *Journal of American History* 80, no 1 (June 1993), 141.

52 "Swimming in the Lincoln Memorial Reflecting Pool," http://www.reddit.com.

53 Frazier, "Recreation and Amusement among American Negroes: A Research Memorandum," unpublished, 1940, 64, Frazier Papers Box 131–74, Folder 1; "District of Columbia–Race and Hispanic Origin: 1800–1990," www.census.gov.

54 The story is recounted in Frazier's *Negro Youth at the Crossways* without naming the young person (to keep it anonymous for the study). A very similar story is told by Susie Morgan in her interview with slightly different information.

55 Frazier, *Negro Youth*, 72.

56 Frazier, *Negro Youth*, 72; Susie Morgan, WDC 22, Frazier Papers, Box 131–112, Folder 11; Box 131–113, Folder 13.

57 Esther (Wright), Frazier Papers, Box 131–112, Folder 12.

58 Simmons, *Crescent City Girls*, 13.

59 "Dunbar Senior Being Tried on Assault Charge," *Washington Tribune*, June 3, 1932; "Student Freed of Rape Charge," *Washington Tribune*, June 10, 1932.

60 See Amber N. Wiley, "The Dunbar High School Dilemma: Architecture, Power, and African American Cultural Heritage," *Buildings and Landscapes* 20, no. 1(Spring 2013): 95–128.

61 Asch and Musgrove, *Chocolate City*, 242.

62 *Washington Tribune*, September 18, 20, 1929; October 11, 1929; June 3, 1932; October 19, 1932; January 13, 1934; April 24, 1937; *Washington Afro-American*, August 13, 1938; September 29, 1939; 1940 United States Census, s.v. "Rama Gibson," "Hazel Hughes."

63 Simmons, *Crescent City Girls*, 12–13.

64 Myron Ross, WDC XIX, Frazier Papers, Box 131–112, Folder 13.

65 Myron Ross, Frazier Papers, Box 131–112, Folder 13.

66 "White Playground in Southwest Washington," Frazier Papers, Box 131–41, Folder 8.

67 Myron Ross, Frazier Papers, Box 131–112, Folder 13.

68 Myron Ross, Frazier Papers, Box 131–112, Folder 13.

69 "Scouts Come to D.C. 500 Strong," *Baltimore Afro-American*, July 3, 1937.

70 "Photonews: 25,000 Scouts from Everywhere Build Tent City in Washington, D.C. for National Jamboree," *Baltimore Afro-American*, July 10, 1937.

71 Myron Ross, Frazier Papers, Box 131–112, Folder 13.

72 Myron Ross, Frazier Papers, Box 131–112, Folder 13.

73 Frazier, *Negro Youth*, 228, 232.

74 Raymond Williams defines "structures of feelings" as "affective elements of consciousness and relationships, [. . .] thought as felt and feelings as thought; practical consciousness [. . .] in a living and interrelating continuity." See Williams, *Marxism and Literature*, specifically chapter 9, "Structures of Feeling."

75 Asch and Musgrove, *Chocolate City*, 238–241.

76 Tract 52, November 30, 1938, Frazier Papers, Box 131–111, Folder 20.

77 Lucy Savage, WDC 45, Frazier Papers, Box 131–113, Folder 10.

78 Jones, *Recreation and Amusement*, 37–44; Willow Tree Playground, Frazier Papers, Box 131–41, Folder 7; Asch and Musgrove, *Chocolate City*, 205; "Annual Report of the Commissioners of the District of Columbia Year Ended June 30, 1921" (Washington: Government Printing Office, 1922), 297–298.

79 Willow Tree Playground, Frazier Papers, Box 131–41, Folder 7.

80 Davies and Derthick, "Race and Social Welfare Policy."

81 "How Washington Protests Police Brutality," *Baltimore Afro-American*, July 16, 1938; "Coffins Barred as Reds March against Police," *Baltimore Afro-American*, July 16, 1938.

82 "Carr's Beach Attracting Many Washingtonians and Baltimoreans," *Washington Tribune*, July 29, 1932.

83 Esther (Wright), third interview, Frazier Papers. "The Speedway" was often someplace that interviewers walked or took the streetcar to in order to conduct the interview. Located in northern SW, where Seventeenth Street NW ended at the Tidal Basin, the Speedway was a part of Potomac Park that included a white-only bathing beach (which had been closed in 1925 due to black protest), tennis courts, a golf course, baseball diamonds, rentable garden plots, polo fields, and places to picnic. Most if not all were either racially restricted or racially segregated.

84 Willow Tree Playground, Frazier Papers, Box 131–41, Folder 7.

85 W.E.B. Du Bois, "Efforts for Social Betterment among Negro Americans" (Atlanta University, 1910), 122–123.

86 "Saves Girl from Gallows: President Wilson Commutes Sentence of Josephine Berry," *Washington Post*, October 15, 1920; "President Saved Girl from Gallows," *Baltimore Afro-American*, October 22, 1920; "D.C. Southwest Community House Result of Dreams of Founder," *Baltimore Afro-American*, November 5, 1932.

87 "Saves Girl from Gallows: President Wilson Commutes Sentence of Josephine Berry," *Washington Post*, October 15, 1920; "President Saved Girl from Gallows," *Baltimore Afro-American*, October 22, 1920; "D.C. Southwest Community House Result of Dreams of Founder," *Baltimore Afro-American*, November 5, 1932.

88 Re: Southwest Settlement House, interview conducted by the only white staff investigator, Ruth J. Bittler, Frazier Papers, 131–112, Folder 8.

89 Re: Southwest Settlement House, Frazier Papers, 131–112, Folder 8; "Saves Girl from Gallows: President Wilson Commutes Sentence of Josephine Berry," *Washington Post*, October 15, 1920; "President Saved Girl from Gallows," *Baltimore Afro-American*, October 22, 1920; "D.C. Southwest Community House Result of Dreams of Founder," *Baltimore Afro-American*, November 5, 1932; "Southwest House," *Baltimore Afro-American*, February 4, 1939.

90 "Mother Child Center Aids Chest Drive," *Baltimore Afro-American*, February 6, 1932; Re: Southwest Settlement House, Frazier Papers, Frazier Papers, 131–112, Folder 8; Nancy F. Cott, *The Grounding of Modern Feminism* (New Haven, CT: Yale University Press, 1987), 85–114.

91 Mothers Health Association flyer, Frazier Papers, Box 131–132, Folder 9.

92 Re: Southwest Settlement House, Frazier Papers, Frazier Papers, 131–112, Folder 8; "Southwest House," *Baltimore Afro-American*, February 4, 1939.

93 Re: Southwest Settlement House, Frazier Papers, Frazier Papers, 131–112, Folder 8.

94 James Richmond, Frazier Papers, Box 131–111, Folder 8.

95 WDC XVIII (James Gray), Frazier Papers, Box 131–74, Folders 3–10 (notecards); Box 131–111, Folders 3–5 (notecards); Box 131–112, Folder 6 (notecards).

96 Life History Rosella, Frazier Papers, Box 131–112, Folder 11; "Notes on Youth Parade," Frazier Papers, Box 131–113, Folder 13.

97 WDC XXV (Harold Jones), Frazier Papers, Box 131–74, Folders 3–10 (notecards); Box 131–111, Folders 3–5 (notecards); Box 131–112, Folder 6 (notecards).

98 Myron Ross, Frazier Papers, Box 131–112, Folder 13.

99 Miller and Gillette, "Race Relations in Washington D.C., 1878–1955," 62–63.

100 "Splendid Columbus Memorial to Be Unveiled in Washington," *New York Times*, June 2, 1912; Asch and Musgrove, *Chocolate City*, 201.

101 WDC XVIII (James Gray), Frazier Papers, Box 131–74, Folders 3–10 (notecards); Box 131–111, Folders 3–5 (notecards); Box 131–112, Folder 6 (notecards).

102 WDC XXVII (Ellsworth Davis), Frazier Papers, Box 131–74 Folders 3–10 (notecards); Box 131–111 Folders 3–5 (notecards); Box 131–112 Folder 6 (notecards).

103 Susie Morgan, Frazier Papers, Box 131–112, Folder 11; Box 131–113, Folder 13.

104 WDC LXXII (Joseph Knight), Frazier Papers, Box 131–74, Folders 3–10 (notecards); Box 131–111, Folders 3–5 (notecards); Box 131–112, Folder 6 (notecards).

105 Miller and Gillette, "Race Relations in Washington D.C., 1878–1955," 64.

106 WDC LXXII (Joseph Knight), Frazier Papers, Box 131–74, Folders 3–10 (notecards); Box 131–111, Folders 3–5 (notecards); Box 131–112, Folder 6 (notecards).

107 Southwest Civil Association, Frazier Papers, Box 131–41, Folder 9.

108 Asch and Musgrove, *Chocolate City*, 298–299.

109 Landis, *Segregation in Washington*, 1–8, 88.

110 Landis, *Segregation in Washington*, 16.

111 Landis, *Segregation in Washington*, 19.

112 Landis, *Segregation in Washington*, 22–23.

113 Landis, *Segregation in Washington*, 21–38.

114 Landis, *Segregation in Washington*, 44–45.

115 Quenton Porter, Frazier Papers, Box 131–113, Folder 9.

116 Susie Morgan to Laura Lee, January 3, 1939, Frazier Papers, Box 131–113, Folder 13.

117 See Sandage, "A Marble House Divided"; Asch and Musgrove, *Chocolate City*, 271.

118 "Porgy and Bess Principals Break D.C. Jim Crow for Run of Show, *Philadelphia Tribune*, March 12, 1936; "Cast Members of 'Porgy and Bess' Block D.C. Jim Crow: Howard Faculty Joins Fight on Discrimination, Theatre Mgr. Forced to Open Houses to All Citizens," *Norfolk New Journal and Guide*, March 14, 1936; "New Gershwin Folks Opera Given First Local Hearing at National," *Washington Post*, March 17, 1936; "Race Bar Falls at D.C. House," *New York Amsterdam News*, March 21, 1936; "Side Seats for Porgy and Bess," *Baltimore Afro-American*, March 21, 1936; Frazier, "Recreation and Amusement among American Negroes," unpublished, 1940, 68–69, Frazier Papers Box 131–74, Folder 1; also see Craig Simpson, "DC's Old Jim Crow Rocked by 1939 Marian Anderson Concert," https://washingtonareaspark.com.

119 Myron Ross, Frazier Papers, Box 131–112, Folder 13.

120 Susie Morgan, Frazier Papers, Box 131–112, Folder 13.

CHAPTER 3. "I WOULD CARRY A SIGN"

1 Holt, "'Story of Ordinary Human Beings,'" 419–420.

2 Description taken from Dennis D. Nelson's interview transcript, "Myron Ross," Frazier Papers, Box 131–112, Folder 13, and from Ted Davis's community report about "A.J. Bowen Playground," Frazier Papers.

3 Myron Ross, Frazier Papers, Box 131–112, Folder 13.

4 Myron Ross, Frazier Papers, Box 131–112, Folder 13.

5 Frazier, *Negro Youth*, 70–79.

6 Frazier, *Negro Youth*, xviii.

7 See Chapter VIII, "Warren Wall," in Frazier, *Negro Youth*, 229.

8 Myron Ross, Frazier Papers, Box 131–112, Folder 13.

9 Myron Ross, Frazier Papers, Box 131–112, Folder 13.

10 Myron Ross, Frazier Papers, Box 131–112, Folder 13.

11 Myron Ross, Frazier Papers, Box 131–112, Folder 13.

12 Myron Ross, Frazier Papers, Box 131–112, Folder 13.

13 Myron Ross, Frazier Papers, Box 131–112, Folder 13.

14 Myron Ross, Frazier Papers, Box 131–112, Folder 13.

15 Myron Ross, Frazier Papers, Box 131–112, Folder 13.

16 Frazier, *Negro Youth*, 264.

17 Myron Ross, Frazier Papers, Box 131–112, Folder 13.

18 Myron Ross, Frazier Papers, Box 131–112, Folder 13.

19 Myron Ross, Frazier Papers, Box 131–112, Folder 13.

20 Myron Ross, Frazier Papers, Box 131–112, Folder 13.

21 Myron Ross, Frazier Papers, Box 131–112, Folder 13.

22 WDC XX1II (William Wright), Frazier Papers, Box 131–74, Folders 3–10 (notecards); Box 131–111, Folders 3–5 (notecards); Box 131–112, Folder 6 (notecards).

23 WDC XX1II (William Wright), Frazier Papers Box 131–74, Folders 3–10 (notecards); 1940 United States Census, s.v. "William Wright," Washington, DC, accessed through Ancestry.com.

24 1940 United States Census, s.v. "Susie Morgan," Washington, DC, accessed through Ancestry.com.

25 Frazier, *Negro Youth*, xvi, xxxiv, 261–262.

26 Anne (Winston), WDC 42, Frazier Papers, Box 131–113, Folder 10.

27 Joseph Ward, Frazier Papers, Box 131–113, Folder 9; Frazier, "Recreation and Amusement among American Negroes," 85–86, Frazier Papers, Box 131–74, Folder 1.

28 See Michele Pacifico's article for not only information on the boycott but on the formation of the New Negro Alliance and the other businesses in DC that they led campaigns against, Pacifico, "'Don't Buy Where You Can't Work'"; Asch and Musgrove, *Chocolate City*, 260–263.

29 Joseph Ward, Frazier Papers, Box 131–113, Folder 9.

30 G. David Houston, "I Walked through a Picket Line," *Washington Afro-American*, August 27, 1938; "Armstrong Principal in Picket Line Controversy," *Washington Afro-American*, September 3, 1938.

31 Gloria Tinner, Frazier Papers, Box 131–112, Folder 10.

32 Bernadyne (Snowden), Frazier Papers, Box 131–112, Folder 10; see Drake's introduction, in *Negro Youth*, xiv–xviii.

33 Verra Couzens does not show up in the census.

34 Verra Couzens, Frazier Papers, Box 131–112, Folder 10.

35 Carolyn Taylor, Frazier Papers, Box 131–112, Folder 10.

36 Minnie and Addie Meade, Frazier Papers, Box 131–112, Folder 10.

37 Alice Williams, WDC 1, Frazier Papers, Box 131–112, Folder 12; Box 131–113 Folder 15; 1920 United States Census, s.v. "Alice Williams," Washington, DC, accessed through Ancestry.com.

38 Alice Williams, WDC 1, Francis Meachum, Frazier Papers, Box 131–112, Folder 12.

39 Drake's introduction, *Negro Youth*, xviii; Frazier, *Negro Youth*, 262.

40 Sullivan, "Chapter IX: A Psychiatric Gloss," 2, in *The Fusion of Psychiatry and Social Science.*

41 Sullivan, "Chapter IX: A Psychiatric Gloss," 2, in *The Fusion of Psychiatry and Social Science.*

CHAPTER 4. "RIGHT TIGHT, RIGHT UNRULY"

1   Susie Morgan, Frazier Papers, Box 131–112, Folder 11; Box 131–113, Folder 13.

2   WDC XVIII (James Gray), Frazier Papers, Box 131–74, Folders 3–10 (notecards); Box 131–111, Folders 3–5 (notecards); Box 131–112, Folder 6 (notecards).

3   1940 United States Census, s.v. "Oscar Morgan," Washington, DC, accessed through Ancestry.com.

4   Susie Morgan, Frazier Papers, Box 131–112, Folder 11; Box 131–113, Folder 13.

5   Susie Morgan, Frazier Papers, Box 131–112, Folder 11; Box 131–113, Folder 13.

6   Susie Morgan, Frazier Papers, Box 131–112, Folder 11; Box 131–113, Folder 13.

7   WDC XVIII (James Gray), Frazier Papers, Box 131–74, Folders 3–10 (notecards); Box 131–111, Folders 3–5 (notecards); Box 131–112, Folder 6 (notecards).

8   James Gray, Frazier Papers, Box 131–74, Folders 3–10; Box 131–111, Folders 3–5; Box 131–112, Folder 6; 1940 United States Census, s.v. "James Gray," Washington, DC, accessed through Ancestry.com.

9   James Gray, Frazier Papers, Box 131–74, Folders 3–10; Box 131–111, Folders 3–5; Box 131–112, Folder 6.

10 Specifically, scholarship that looks at early free black communities in the United States addresses this, including Craig Steven Wilder, *In the Company of Men: The African Influence on African American Culture in New York City* (New York: New York University Press, 2001); Leslie Alexander, *African or American? Black Identity and Political Activism in New York City, 1784–1861* (Urbana: University of Illinois Press, 2008); Shane White, *Somewhat More Independent: The End of Slavery in New York City, 1770–1810* (Athens: University of Georgia Press, 1991); and Graham Russell Hodges, *Root and Branch: African Americans in New York and East Jersey, 1613–1863* (Chapel Hill: University of North Carolina Press, 1999), to name just a few.

11 James Gray, Frazier Papers, Box 131–74, Folders 3–10; Box 131–111, Folders 3–5; Box 131–112, Folder 6.

12 James Gray, Frazier Papers, Box 131–74, Folders 3–10; Box 131–111, Folders 3–5; Box 131–112, Folder 6.

13 James Gray, Frazier Papers, Box 131–74, Folders 3–10; Box 131–111, Folders 3–5; Box 131–112, Folder 6.

14 Frazier, "Recreation and Amusement among American Negroes," unpublished, 1940, 86, Frazier Papers. In the full quote, Frazier states that in DC's "slum areas" there is a low level of literacy among poor and working-class black parents and that as a result, young people, despite being "exposed to formal instruction [. . .] seldom acquire a taste for reading as a form of recreation," except for "salacious types of reading matter," like the magazines *True Stories* and *True Romances*.

15 James Gray, Frazier Papers, Box 131–74, Folders 3–10; Box 131–111, Folders 3–5; Box 131–112, Folder 6.

16 See Driscoll, *Girls*, 74–76.

17 James Gray, Frazier Papers, Box 131–74, Folders 3–10; Box 131–111, Folders 3–5; Box 131–112, Folder 6.

18 James Gray, Frazier Papers, Box 131–74, Folders 3–10; Box 131–111, Folders 3–5; Box 131–112, Folder 6.

19 See Bederman, *Manliness and Civilization*, 17–20; Summers, *Manliness and Its Discontents*, 152–153, 173; see also Roderick Ferguson's review of Marlon Ross's *Manning the Race* and Summer's *Manliness and Its Discontents* in "African American Masculinity and the Study of Social Formations," *American Quarterly* 58, no. 1 (March 2006): 213–219.

20 Stanley Russell (XXIX), Frazier Papers, Box 131–74, Folders 3–10 (notecards); Box 131–111, Folders 3–5 (notecards); Box 131–112, Folder 6 (notecards).

21 Stanley Russell, Frazier Papers, Box 131–74, Folders 3–10; Box 131–111, Folders 3–5; Box 131–112, Folder 6.

22 Stanley Russell, Frazier Papers, Box 131–74, Folders 3–10; Box 131–111, Folders 3–5; Box 131–112, Folder 6.

23 Stanley Russell, Frazier Papers, Box 131–74, Folders 3–10; Box 131–111, Folders 3–5; Box 131–112, Folder 6.

24 Stanley Russell, Frazier Papers, Box 131–74, Folders 3–10; Box 131–111, Folders 3–5; Box 131–112, Folder 6.

25 Ruth J. Bittler, "Soap Box Derby," July 23, 1938, Frazier Papers, 131–112, Folder 10.

26 Wolcott, *Cops and Kids*, 35–38; see also Aimee Meredith Cox's introduction to *Shapeshifters*.

27 Frazier, "Recreation and Amusement among American Negroes," 85–86, Frazier Papers, Box 131–74, Folder 1.

28 See the discussion of Quenton Porter's mother's support of her son's participation in both a gang and approved-of recreation activities in chapter 2.

29 Hoyte Scott (XXIV), Frazier Papers, Box 131–74, Folders 3–10 (notecards); Box 131–111, Folders 3–5 (notecards); Box 131–112, Folder 6 (notecards).

30 1930 and 1940 United States Census, s.v. "Hoyt Scott," Washington, DC, accessed through Ancestry.com; Frazier, *Negro Youth*, 24–25.

31 Hoyte Scott, Frazier Papers, Box 131–74, Folders 3–10; Box 131–111, Folders 3–5; Box 131–112, Folder 6.

32 Hoyte Scott, Frazier Papers, Box 131–74, Folders 3–10; Box 131–111, Folders 3–5; Box 131–112, Folder 6.

33 Nathaniel Smith (XVI), Frazier Papers, Box 131–74, Folders 3–10 (notecards); Box 131–111, Folders 3–5 (notecards); Box 131–112, Folder 6 (notecards).

34 Nathaniel Smith, Frazier Papers, Box 131–74, Folders 3–10; Box 131–111, Folders 3–5; Box 131–112, Folder 6.

35 Nathaniel Smith, Frazier Papers, Box 131–74, Folders 3–10; Box 131–111, Folders 3–5; Box 131–112, Folder 6.

36 See Summers, *Manliness and Its Discontents*.

37 Nathaniel Smith, Frazier Papers, Box 131–74, Folders 3–10; Box 131–111, Folders 3–5; Box 131–112, Folder 6.

38 Nathaniel Smith, Frazier Papers, Box 131–74, Folders 3–10; Box 131–111, Folders 3–5; Box 131–112, Folder 6.

39 Constance M. Green, *Washington, a History of the Capital, 1800–1950* (Princeton, NJ: Princeton University Press, 1977), 158; Sacks, "Honor among Criminals?," 249. Sacks was in the School of Social Work at Catholic University.

40 Nathaniel Smith, Frazier Papers, Box 131–74, Folders 3–10; Box 131–111, Folders 3–5; Box 131–112, Folder 6.

41 Nathaniel Smith, Frazier Papers, Box 131–74, Folders 3–10; Box 131–111, Folders 3–5; Box 131–112, Folder 6.

42 1930 and 1940 United States Census, s.v. "Nathaniel Smith," Washington, DC, accessed through Ancestry.com.

43 Joseph Knight (LXXXII), Frazier Papers, Box 131–74, Folders 3–10 (notecards); Box 131–111, Folders 3–5 (notecards); Box 131–112, Folder 6 (notecards).

44 Joseph Knight, Frazier Papers, Box 131–74, Folders 3–10; Box 131–111, Folders 3–5; Box 131–112, Folder 6.

45 Joseph Knight, Frazier Papers, Box 131–74, Folders 3–10; Box 131–111, Folders 3–5; Box 131–112, Folder 6; "Willow Tree Playground, July 21, 1938," Frazier Papers, Box 131–41, Folder 7. Willow Tree Playground was one of Southwest's only playgrounds that was open year-round; it was situated in the square of Third, Fourth, D Street, and Independence Avenue, abutting the National Mall. See chapter 2 for a discussion of its formation and eventual replacement by federal buildings.

46 Joseph Knight, Frazier Papers, Box 131–74, Folders 3–10; Box 131–111, Folders 3–5; Box 131–112, Folder 6.

47 Life History, Rosella Hillman, Frazier Papers, Box 131–112, Folder 11.

48 "Group Interaction at Southwest House, May 9th, 1938," Frazier Papers, Box 131–113, Folder 4.

49 Susie Morgan, Frazier Papers, Box 131–112, Folder 11; Box 131–113, Folder 13.

50 Susie Morgan, Frazier Papers, Box 131–112, Folder 11; Box 131–113, Folder 13.

51 Frazier, *Negro Youth*, 78.

52 Myron Ross, Frazier Papers, Box 131–112, Folder 13; Alice Williams, Frazier Papers, Box 131–112, Folder 12; James Richmond, Frazier Papers, Box 131–111, Folder 8.

53 Susie Morgan, Frazier Papers, Box 131–112, Folder 11; Box 131–113, Folder 13.

54 Esther Wright, Frazier Papers, Box 131–112, Folder 11; Box 131–113, Folder 13.

55 Lucy Savage, Frazier Papers, Box 131–112, Folder 11; Box 131–113, Folder 13.

56 Lucy Savage, Frazier Papers, Box 131–112, Folder 11; Box 131–113, Folder 13; also see Constance Green, *Washington, a History of the Capital, 1800–1950* (Princeton, NJ: Princeton University Press, 1977), for more on the Occoquan workhouse in Virginia.

57 Lucy Savage, Frazier Papers, Box 131–112, Folder 11; Box 131–113, Folder 13.

58 Rosella Hillman, Frazier Papers, Box 131–112, Folder 11.

59 Rosella Hillman, Frazier Papers, Box 131–112, Folder 11.

60 Martha Harris, Frazier Papers, Box 131–112, Folder 11.

61 Alice Williams, Frazier Papers, Box 131–112, Folder 12; Box 131–113, Folder 15.

62 "Organization Committee of WTUL, May 19, 1938," Frazier Papers, Box 131–113, Folder 5.

63 Anne Winston, Frazier Papers, Box 131–113, Folder 10; "Meeting of the Organization Committee of the Women's Trade Union League, June 10, 1938," Frazier Papers, Box 131–113, Folder 5.

64 The interview with Belt appears in the papers for "Henrietta Hinton WDC 47" who was Belt's younger niece and the intended interviewee. Henrietta Hinton, WDC 47, Frazier Papers, Box 131–111, Box 8.

65 Henrietta Belt, Frazier Papers, Box 131–111, Box 8.

66 James Richmond, Frazier Papers, Box 131–111, Folder 8.

67 Here I reference Susan Cahn's use of Walter Benjamin's "wish images," "utopian imagination" that gestured toward a future "emancipatory reality." Cahn posits that expectations expressed by the young women in Charles S. Johnson's study were "imagined futures" that represented young people's understandings of their own capacities for achievement, and "entitlement to having more"—"more power to shape their lives." Cahn, *Sexual Reckonings*, 127, 336 n37.

CONCLUSION

1 Parks, *Choice of Weapons*, 217–220.

2 Parks, *Choice of Weapons*, 222–225.

3 Parks, *Choice of Weapons*, 232.

4 Landis, *Segregation in Washington*, 1–8.

5 Landis, *Segregation in Washington*, 60.

6 Landis, *Segregation in Washington*, 54–58.

7 Sandage, "A Marble House Divided," 147.

8 Landis, *Segregation in Washington*, 88.

9 Asch and Musgrove, *Chocolate City*, 292.

10 Asch and Musgrove, *Chocolate City*, 300–301.

11 Asch and Musgrove, *Chocolate City*, 285–287.

12 Asch and Musgrove, *Chocolate City*, 320–325; Ammon, "Commemoration amid Criticism," 202.

13 Daniel Thursz, Where Are They Now?, chapter 2, "Characteristics of the Families in Old Southwest," 19.

14 Daniel Thursz, Where Are They Now?, tables 11, 12, 13, 14, pages 58–63; Keith Melder, "Southwest Washington: Where History Stopped," in *Washington at Home*, ed. Smith, 99–100.

15 Thursz, Where Are They Now?, 65.

16 Thursz, Where Are They Now?, 66–70, 100; Melder, "Southwest Washington: Where History Stopped," in *Washington at Home*, ed. Smith, 99.

17 Hartman, "Venus in Two Acts," 13.

18 Hartman, "Venus in Two Acts," 3, 12.

19 Frazier, "Negro Middle Class and Desegregation," 291–301.

20 Frazier, *Negro Youth*, 275.

21 Frazier argues against William McDougall's assertion, in his *Is America Safe for Democracy?* (1921), that African Americans and more generally all people of African descent have a particularly "strong submissive *instinct*." McDougall was a psychologist interested in employing a kind of anthropological psychology in the service of eugenics. See McDougall, *Is America Safe for Democracy?*, 117–118.

22 St. Clair Drake, "Introduction to the 1967 Edition," *Negro Youth*, xiii.

23 Quashie, *Sovereignty of Quiet*, 134.

24 Asch and Musgrove, *Chocolate City*, 305–308.

25 Asch and Musgrove, *Chocolate City*, 300–302.

26 Asch and Musgrove, *Chocolate City*, 338.

27 Asch and Musgrove, *Chocolate City*, 347–351.

28 http://www.huffingtonpost.com.

29 Quashie, *Sovereignty of Quiet*, 134.

BIBLIOGRAPHY

PRIMARY SOURCES

Manuscript and Archive Collections

MOORLAND-SPINGARN RESEARCH CENTER, HOWARD UNIVERSITY, WASHINGTON, DC

E. Franklin Frazier Papers

Baker's Dozen Papers

Thomas Wyatt Turner Papers

Works Progress Administration (WPA) collection

NATIONAL ARCHIVES

Records of the National Capital Housing Authority, photographs/slides 1916–38

WASHINGTON, D.C. HISTORICAL SOCIETY

Washington, DC, city planning maps

LIBRARY OF CONGRESS

Nannie Helen Burroughs National Training School for Women and Girls, student records

WPA Records for District of Columbia

Washington, DC, street photographs, Farm Security Administration

Sanborn Fire Insurance and Real Estate Plat Maps

SCHOMBURG CENTER FOR RESEARCH IN BLACK CULTURE, NEW YORK PUBLIC LIBRARY

Farm Security Administration, Washington, DC, photographs

Periodicals (some are available digitally through the New York Public Library or at the Washingtoniana Collection at the Washington, DC, Martin Luther King, Jr. Public Library)

Baltimore Afro-American

Evening Star

Evening Sun

New York Times

Nitelife

The Crisis

Washington Afro-American

Washington Bee

Washington Post

Washington Star

Washington Sun

Washington Tribune

Published

Baker, Ray Stannard. *Following the Color Line: American Negro Citizenship in the Progressive Era*. New York: Harper & Row, 1908.

Bartlett, Harriet M. "The Social Survey and the Charity Organization Movement." *American Journal of Sociology* 34, no. 2 (September 1928): 330–346.

Dabney, Lillian Gertrude. *The History of Schools for Negroes in the District of Columbia: 1807–1947*. Washington, DC: Catholic University Press, 1949.

Davis, Allison, and John Dollard. *Children of Bondage: The Personality Development of Negro Youth in the Urban South*. Washington, DC: American Council on Education, 1940. Reprint, New York: Harper & Row, 1964.

Du Bois, W. E. B. *Darkwater: Voices from within the Veil*. New York: Harcourt, Brace, & Co., 1920. Reprint, New York: Oxford University Press, 2007.

———. *Dusk of Dawn: An Essay toward an Autobiography of Race Concept*. New York: Harcourt, Brace, & Co., 1940.

———. *The Philadelphia Negro: A Social Study*. Philadelphia: University of Pennsylvania Press, 1899. Reprint, Philadelphia: University of Pennsylvania Press, 1996.

———. "The Secret City: An Impression of Colored Washington, D.C." *The Crisis* (June 1932): 185–187.

———. *The Souls of Black Folks*. Chicago: A. C. McClurg & Co., 1903. Reprint, New York: Oxford University Press, 2007.

Dyson, Walter. *Howard University, the Capstone of Negro Education: A History: 1867–1940*. Washington, DC: Graduate School of Howard University, 1941.

Frazier, E. Franklin. *The Negro Family in the United States*. Notre Dame, IN: University of Notre Dame Press, 1939. Reprint, Notre Dame, IN: University of Notre Dame Press, 2001.

———. "The Negro Middle Class and Desegregation." *Social Problems* 4, no. 4 (April 1957): 291–301.

———. *Negro Youth at the Crossways: Their Personality Development in the Middle States.* Washington, DC: American Council on Education, 1940. Reprint, New York: Schocken Books, 1967.

———. "The Pathology of Race Prejudice." *Forum* (June 1927): 856–861.

"Harlem: Mecca of the New Negro." Special issue of *Survey Graphic* 6, no. 6 (March 1925): 621–724.

Huddleson, Sarah M. "The Sunny Southwest." *Records of the Columbia Historical Society, Washington, D.C.* 26 (1924): 157–187.

Johnson, Charles S. *Growing Up in the Black Belt: Negro Youth in the Rural South.* Washington, DC: American Council on Education, 1941.

Jones, Thomas Jesse. *Directory of Inhabited Alleys of Washington, D.C.* Washington, DC: Monday Evening Club, 1912.

Jones, William H. *The Housing of Negroes in Washington, D.C.: A Study in Human Ecology.* Washington, DC: Washington Federation of Churches, 1929.

———. *Recreation and Amusement among Negroes in Washington D.C.: A Sociological Analysis of the Negro in an Urban Environment.* Washington, DC: Howard University Press, 1927.

Locke, Alain. "Enter the New Negro." In "Harlem: Mecca of the New Negro," special issue of *Survey Graphic* 6, no. 6 (March 1925): 631–634.

———. *The New Negro: An Interpretation.* New York: Albert and Charles Boni, 1925.

Logan, Rayford W., ed. *What the Negro Wants.* Chapel Hill: University of North Carolina Press, 1944.

McDougall, William. *Is America Safe for Democracy: Six Lectures Given at Lowell Institute of Boston under the Title of "Anthropology and History or Influence of Anthropologic Constitution on the Destinies of Nations."* New York: Scribner and Sons, 1921.

Miller, Kelly. "Where Is the Negro's Heaven?" *Opportunity* (December 1926). In *Opportunity Reader: Stories, Poetry, and Essays from the Urban League's Opportunity Magazine,* edited by Sondra K. Wilson, 425–426. New York: Modern Library, 1999.

Moynihan, Daniel Patrick. *The Negro Family: The Case for National Action.* Washington, DC: US Department of Labor, Office of Policy Planning and Research, 1968.

Myrdal, Gunnar. *An American Dilemma: The Negro Problem and Modern Democracy.* New York: Harper and Row, 1944.

Parks, Gordon. *A Choice of Weapons.* New York: Harper & Row, 1966.

Reid, Ira De A. *In a Minor Key: Negro Youth in Story and Fact.* Washington, DC: American Council on Education, 1940.

———. *The Negro Immigrant: His Background, Characteristics, and Social Adjustment, 1899–1937.* New York: Columbia University Press, 1939.

Riis, Jacob. *How the Other Half Lives: Studies among the Tenements of New York.* New York: Scribner, 1890.

Sacks, Jerome G. "Honor among Criminals?" *Journal of Criminal Law and Criminology* 28, no. 2 (July–August 1937): 249–252.

Segregation in Washington: A Report of the National Committee on Segregation in the Nation's Capital. Chicago: National Committee on Segregation in the Nation's Capital, 1948.

Sullivan, Harry Stack. *The Fusion of Psychiatry and Social Science.* New York: William Alanson White Psychiatric Foundation, 1964.

Sutherland, Robert L. *Color, Class, and Personality.* Washington, DC: American Council on Education, 1942.

Taeuber, Karl E., Leonard Chiazze Jr., and William Haenszel. *Migration in the United States: An Analysis of Residence Histories.* Washington, DC: Department of Health, Education and Welfare, 1968.

Terrell, Mary Church. *A Colored Woman in a White World.* Washington, DC: Ransdell, 1940.

Warner, W. Lloyd. *Color and Human Nature: Negro Personality Development in a Northern City.* Washington, DC: American Council on Education, 1941.

Washington: City and Capital Federal Writer's Project Works Project Administration American Guide Series. Washington, DC: Government Printing Office, 1937.

Weller, Charles F. *Neglected Neighbors: Stories of Life in the Alleys, Tenements, and Shanties of the National Capital.* Philadelphia: John C. Winston Co., 1909.

Wirth, Louis. "The Ideological Aspects of Social Disorganization." *American Sociological Review* 5, no. 4 (August 1940): 472–482.

The WPA Guide to Washington, D.C.: The Federal Writer's Project Guide to 1930s Washington. Washington, DC: Government Printing Office, 1942.

Master's Theses and Dissertations

Dewhirst, Edith Ward. "Recreational Opportunities for the Adolescent Girl in Washington, D.C." MA thesis, George Washington University, 1942.

Johnson, Gwendolyn. "The Transformation of Juvenile Gangs into Accommodated Groups: A Study of Eight Boys' Gangs in Washington, D.C." MA thesis, Howard University, 1949.

Mason, Natalie. "A Study of the Supervision of Twenty-Five Parolees from a Training School for Girls Immediately Preceding Their Internment and Problems Confronting Them upon Release." MSW thesis, Howard University, 1951.

Mugrauer, Bertha. "A Cultural Study of Ten Negro Girls in an Alley." PhD diss., Catholic University, 1950.

Ober, Dorothy. "The Social Hygiene Society of Washington, D.C. from 1933–1940: Study of the Adjustment of a Community Organization to Changing Conditions." MA thesis, Howard University, 1951.

Ratigan, Marion. "A Sociological Survey of Disease in Four Alleys in the National Capital." PhD diss., Catholic University of America, 1946.

Sellew, Gladys. "A Deviant Social Situation: A Court." PhD diss., Catholic University of America, 1938.

Somerville, Dora Bessie. "A Study of a Group of Negro Children Living in an Alley Culture." MA thesis, Catholic University of America, 1941.

SECONDARY SOURCES

Abbott, Carl. *Political Terrain: Washington, D.C., from Tidewater Town to Global Metropolis.* Chapel Hill: University of North Carolina Press, 1999.

Abernathy, Lloyd M. "The Washington Race War." *Maryland Historical Magazine* 58 (1963): 309–324.

Alexander, Elizabeth. *The Black Interior.* St. Paul, MN: Graywolf Press, 2004.

Ammon, Francesca Russello. "Commemoration amid Criticism: The Mixed Legacy of Urban Renewal in Southwest Washington, D.C." *Journal of Planning History* 8, no. 3 (August 2009): 175–220.

Asch, Chris Myers, and George Derek Musgrove. *Chocolate City: A History of Race and Democracy in the Nation's Capital.* Chapel Hill: University of North Carolina Press, 2017.

Baker, Lee D. *Anthropology and the Racial Politics of Culture.* Durham, NC: Duke University Press, 2010.

———. *From Savage to Negro: Anthropology and the Construction of Race, 1896–1954.* Berkeley: University of California Press, 1998.

Barnes, William R. "Battle for Washington: Ideology, Racism, and Self-Interest in the Controversy over Public Housing, 1943–1946." *Columbia Historical Society* 50 (1980): 452–483.

Bay, Mia. *The White Image in the Black Mind: African American Ideas about White People, 1830–1925.* New York: Oxford University Press, 2000.

Bay, Mia, Farah J. Griffin, Martha S. Jones, and Barbara D. Savage, eds. *Toward an Intellectual History of Black Women.* Chapel Hill: University of North Carolina Press, 2015.

Bederman, Gail. *Manliness and Civilization: A Cultural History of Gender and Race in the United States, 1880–1917.* Chicago: University of Chicago Press, 1995.

Bellesile, Michael A., ed. *Lethal Imagination: Violence and Brutality in American History.* New York: New York University Press, 1999.

Bernstein, Robin. *Racial Innocence: Performing American Childhood from Slavery to Civil Rights.* New York: New York University Press, 2011.

Best, Wallace D. *Passionately Human, No Less Divine: Religion and Culture in Black Chicago, 1915–1952.* Princeton, NJ: Princeton University Press, 2005.

Black Public Sphere Collective, ed. *The Black Public Sphere.* Chicago: University of Chicago Press, 1995.

Borchert, James. *Alley Life in Washington: Family, Community, Religion, and Folklife in the City, 1850–1970.* Urbana: University of Illinois Press, 1980.

Brewer, Rose. "Theorizing Race, Class and Gender: The New Scholarship on Black Feminist Intellectuals and Black Women's Labor." In *Theorizing Black Feminisms: The Visionary Pragmatism of Black Women,* edited by Stanlie M. James and Abena P. A. Busia. New York: Routledge Press, 1993.

Brown, Ruth Nicole. *Hear Our Truths: The Creative Potential of Black Girlhood.* Urbana: University of Illinois Press, 2013.

———. "Speaking Freely and Fully: The Political Significance of Black Girls' Way with Words." *International Journal of Africana Studies* 13, no. 1 (Spring 2007): 82–98.

Burgett, Bruce, and Glenn Hendler, eds. *Keywords for American Cultural Studies*. New York: New York University Press, 2007.

Cahn, Susan H. *Sexual Reckonings: Southern Girls in a Troubling Age*. Cambridge, MA: Harvard University Press, 2007.

Caldwell, Roberta. "The Washington Riot of 1919." MA thesis, Howard University, 1971.

Calhoun, Craig, ed. *Sociology in America: A History*. Chicago: University of Chicago Press, 2007.

Campt, Tina. *Listening to Images*. Durham, NC: Duke University Press, 2017.

Cantwell, Thomas. "Anacostia: Strength in Adversity." *Records of the Columbia Historical Society* 73–74 (1976): 330–370.

Carby, Hazel. "Policing the Black Woman's Body in an Urban Context." *Critical Inquiry* 18 (Summer 1992): 738–755.

———. *Race Men*. Cambridge, MA: Harvard University Press, 1998.

Carlson, Shirley J. "Black Ideals of Womanhood in the Late Victorian Era." *Journal of Negro History* 77, no. 2 (Spring 1992): 61–73.

Cary, Francine Curry, ed. *Urban Odyssey: A Multicultural History of Washington, D.C.* Washington, DC: Smithsonian Institution Press, 1996.

Chafe, William, ed. *Remembering Jim Crow: African Americans Tell about Life in the Segregated South*. New York: New Press, 2001.

Chatelain, Marcia. "'The Most Interesting Girl in This Country Is the Colored Girl': Girls and Racial Uplift in Great Migration Chicago, 1899–1950." PhD diss., Brown University, 2008.

———. *South Side Girls: Growing Up in the Great Migration*. Durham, NC: Duke University Press, 2015.

Chauncey, George. *Gay New York: Gender, Urban Culture, and the Making of the Gay Male World 1890–1940*. New York: Basic Books, 1994.

Clark-Lewis, Elizabeth. *Living In, Living Out: African American Domestics in Washington, D.C., 1910–1940*. Washington, DC: Smithsonian Institution Press, 1994.

Cohen, Lizabeth. *Making a New Deal: Industrial Workers in Chicago, 1919–1939*. New York: Cambridge University Press, 1990.

Collins, Donald. "A Substance of Things Hoped For: Multiculturalism, Desegregation, and Identity in African American Washington, D.C., 1930–1960." PhD diss., Carnegie Mellon University, 1997.

Cox, Aimee Meredith. *Shapeshifters: Black Girls and the Choreography of Citizenship*. Durham, NC: Duke University Press, 2015.

Curwood, Anastasia. *Stormy Weather: Middle Class African American Marriages between the Two World Wars*. Chapel Hill: University of North Carolina Press, 2010.

Davies, Gareth, and Martha Derthick. "Race and Social Welfare Policy: The Social Security Act of 1935." *Political Science Quarterly* 112, no. 2 (Summer 1997): 217–235.

Delany, David. *Race, Place, and the Law, 1836–1948*. Austin: University of Texas, 1998.

Delany, Samuel R. *Times Square Red, Times Square Blue*. New York: New York University Press, 1999.

Digital Harlem: Everyday Life 1915–1930. http://acl.arts.usyd.edu.au/harlem/.

Dill, Bonnie Thornton. "The Dialectics of Black Womanhood." *Signs* 4, no. 3 (Spring 1979): 543–555.

Driscoll, Catherine. *Girls: Feminine Adolescence in Popular Culture and Cultural Theory*. New York: Columbia University Press, 2002.

Edwards, Laura F. *Gendered Strife and Confusion: The Political Culture of Reconstruction*. Champaign: University of Illinois Press, 1997.

Ellickson, Robert C. "Controlling Chronic Misconduct in City Spaces: Of Panhandlers, Skid Rows, and Public Space Zoning." *Yale Law Journal* 105, no. 5 (March 1996): 1165–1248.

Fass, Paula. "Cultural History/Social History: Some Reflections on a Continuing Dialogue." *Journal of Social History* 37, no. 1 (Fall 2003): 39–46.

Favor, Martin J. *Authentic Blackness: The Folk in the New Negro Renaissance*. Durham, NC: Duke University Press, 1999.

Feld, Barry C. *Bad Kids: Race and the Transformation of the Juvenile Court*. New York: Oxford University Press, 1999.

Feldstein, Ruth. *Motherhood in Black and White: Race and Sex in American Liberalism 1930–1965*. Ithaca, NY: Cornell University Press, 2000.

Field, Corinne T., Tammy-Cherelle Owens, Marcia Chatelain, LaKisha Simmons, Abosede George, and Rhian Keyse. "The History of Black Childhood: Recent Innovations and Future Directions." *Journal of the History of Childhood and Youth* 9, no. 3 (Fall 2016): 383–401.

Foley, Barbara. *Spectres of 1919: Class and Nation in Making of the New Negro*. Urbana: University of Illinois Press, 2003.

Gagne, Karen M. "On the Obsolescence of the Disciplines: Frantz Fanon and Sylvia Wynter Propose a New Mode of Being Human." *Human Architecture: Journal of the Sociology of Self-Knowledge* 5, no. 3 (2007): 1–13.

Gaines, Kevin. *Uplifting the Race: Black Leadership, Politics, and Culture in the Twentieth Century*. Chapel Hill: University of North Carolina Press, 1996.

Gardullo, Paul, Michelle Delaney, Jacquelyn D. Serwer, and Lonnie G. Bunch III, eds. *Picturing the Promise: The Scurlock Studio and Black Washington*. Washington, DC: National Museum of African American History and Culture, Smithsonian Institution, 2009.

Gillette, Howard, Jr. *Between Justice and Beauty: Race, Planning, and the Failure of Urban Policy in Washington, D.C.* Baltimore: Johns Hopkins University Press, 1995.

Gilmore, Ruth Wilson. "Fatal Couplings of Power and Difference: Notes on Racism and Geography." *Professional Geographer* 54, no. 1 (2002): 15–24.

Goings, Kenneth, and Raymond A. Mohl, eds. *The New African American Urban History*. Thousand Oaks, CA: Sage Publications, 1996.

Gordon, Linda. *Pitied but Not Entitled: Single Mothers and the History of Welfare, 1890–1935*. New York: Free Press, 1994.

Gottlieb, Peter. *Making Their Way: Southern Blacks' Migration to Pittsburgh, 1916–1930*. Urbana-Champaign: University of Illinois Press, 1987.

Green, Constance M. *The Secret City: A History of Race Relations in the Nation's Capital*. Princeton, NJ: Princeton University Press, 1967.

———. *Washington, a History of the Capital, 1800–1950*. Princeton, NJ: Princeton University Press, 1977.

Grossman, James. *Land of Hope: Chicago, Black Southerners, and the Great Migration*. Chicago: University of Chicago Press, 1989.

Groves, Paul A. "The Development of a Black Residential Community in Southwest Washington: 1860–1897." *Records of the Columbia Historical Society, Washington, D.C.* 49 (1973–74): 260–275.

Hannold, Elizabeth. "Comfort and Respectability: Washington's Philanthropic Housing Movement." *Washington History* 4, no. 2 (Fall/Winter 1992–93): 20–39.

Harley, Sharon. "Beyond the Classroom: The Organizational Lives of Black Female Educators in the District of Columbia, 1890–1930." *Journal of Negro Education* 51, no. 3 (Summer 1982): 254–265.

———. "When Your Work Is Not Who You Are: The Development of a Working Class Consciousness among Afro-American Women." In *Gender, Class, Race, and Reform in the Progressive Era*, edited by Noralee Frankel and Nancy S. Dye. Lexington: University of Kentucky Press, 1991.

Harper, Phillip Brian. *"Are We Not Men?" Masculine Anxiety and the Problem of African American Identity*. New York: Oxford University Press, 1996.

Harris, Jennifer. "Reading Mobility, Motherhood, and Domesticity in Four African American Women's Texts." *Journal of the Association for Research on Mothering* 2, no. 2 (2000): 200–210.

Harrison, Michael R. "The 'Evil of the Misfit Subdivisions': Creating the Permanent System of Highways of the District of Columbia." *Washington History* 14, no. 1 (Spring–Summer 2002): 26–55.

Hartman, Saidiya. "Venus in Two Acts." *Small Axe* 26 (June 2008): 1–14.

———. *Wayward Lives, Beautiful Experiments: Intimate Histories of Social Upheaval*. New York: W. W. Norton, 2019.

Harvey, David. "The Right to the City." *New Left Review* 53 (September–October 2008): 23–40.

Hawes, Joseph M. *Children between the Wars: American Childhood, 1920–1940*. New York: Twayne Publishers, 1997.

Hawes, Joseph M., and N. Ray Hiner, eds. *American Childhood: A Research Guide and Historical Handbook*. Westport, CT: Greenwood Press, 1985.

Hicks, Cheryl. *Talk with You Like a Woman: Women, Justice, and Reform in New York, 1890–1935*. Chapel Hill: University of North Carolina Press, 2010.

Higginbotham, Evelyn Brooks. "African-American Women's History and the Metalanguage of Race." *Signs: Journal of Women in Culture and Society* 17 (Spring 1992): 251–274.

Hine, Darlene Clark. "African American Women and Their Communities in the Twentieth Century." *Black Women, Gender, and Families* 1, no. 1 (Spring 2007): 1–23.

———. "Black Migration to the Urban Midwest: The Gender Dimension 1915–1945." In *The Great Migration in Historical Perspective: New Dimensions of Race, Class, and Gender*, edited by Joe W. Trotter Jr. Bloomington: Indiana University Press, 1991.

———. "Rape and the Inner Lives of Southern Black Women: Thoughts on the Culture of Dissemblance." In *Southern Women: Histories and Identities*, edited by Virginia Bernhard, Betty Brandon, Elizabeth Fox-Genovese, and Theda Purdue. Columbia: University of Missouri Press, 1992.

Hine, Darlene Clark, and Earnestine Jenkins, eds. *A Question of Manhood: A Reader in U.S. Black Men's History and Masculinity*, vol. 2, *The 19th Century: From Emancipation to Jim Crow*. Bloomington: Indiana University Press, 2001.

Holloway, Jonathan Scott. *Confronting the Veil: Abram Harris, Jr., E. Franklin Frazier, and Ralph Bunche, 1919–1941*. Chapel Hill: University of North Carolina Press, 2002.

Holt, Thomas. "'A Story of Ordinary Human Beings': The Sources of Du Bois's Historical Imagination." In "Du Bois's *Black Reconstruction*: Past and Present," edited by Thavolia Glymph, a special issue of *South Atlantic Quarterly* 112, no. 3 (2013): 419–420.

Hunter, Tera W. *To 'Joy My Freedom: Southern Black Women's Lives and Labors after the Civil War*. Cambridge, MA: Harvard University Press, 1997.

Jarmon, Charles. "E. Franklin Frazier's Sociology of Race and Class in Black America." *Black Scholar* 43 (April 2013): 89–102.

Johnson, Ronald M. "Black and White Apart: The Community Center Movement in the District of Columbia, 1915–1930." *Columbia Historical Society* 52 (1989): 1–11.

Johnson, Walter. "On Agency." *Journal of Social History* 37, no. 1 (Autumn 2003): 113–124.

Jones, Edward P. *All Aunt Hagar's Children*. New York: Harper Collins, 2006.

———. *Lost in the City*. New York: Harper Collins, 1992.

Jones, William P. *The Tribe of Black Ulysses: African American Lumber Workers in the Jim Crow South*. Champaign-Urbana: University of Illinois Press, 2005.

Kahrl, Andrew W. *Land Was Ours: African American Beaches from Jim Crow to the Sunbelt South*. Cambridge, MA: Harvard University Press, 2012.

———. "On the Beach: Race and Leisure in the Jim Crow South." PhD diss., Indiana University, 2008.

Katz, Michael B., and Thomas J. Sugrue, eds. *W. E. B. Du Bois, Race, and the City: The Philadelphia Negro and Its Legacy*. Philadelphia: University of Pennsylvania Press, 1998.

Kelley, Robin D. G. *Yo Mama Is Disfunktional! Fighting the Culture Wars in Urban America*. Boston: Beacon Press, 1997.

King, Wilma. *African American Childhoods: Historical Perspectives from Slavery to Civil Rights*. New York: Palgrave Macmillan, 2005.

———. *Stolen Childhood: Slave Youth in Nineteenth-Century America*. Bloomington: Indiana University Press, 1995.

Kofie, Nelson F. *Race, Class, and the Struggle for Neighborhood in Washington, D.C.* Westport, CT: Praeger, 2003.

Ladner, Joyce A., ed. *The Death of White Sociology: Essays on Race and Culture.* Baltimore: Black Classic Press, [1973] 1998.

Lamothe, Daphne. *Inventing the New Negro: Narrative, Culture, and Ethnography.* Philadelphia: University of Pennsylvania Press, 2008.

Lasch-Quinn, Elizabeth. *Black Neighbors: Race and the Limits of Reform in the American Settlement House Movement, 1890–1945.* Chapel Hill: University of North Carolina Press, 1993.

Leach, William. *Land of Desire: Merchants, Power, and the Rise of a New American Culture.* New York: Vintage, 1994.

Lewis, David Levering. *District of Columbia: A Bicentennial History.* New York: W. W. Norton, 1976.

Lewis, Earl. *In Their Own Interests: Race, Class, and Power in Twentieth-Century Norfolk, Virginia.* Berkeley: University of California Press, 1993.

Lindenmeyer, Kriste. *The Greatest Generation Grows Up: American Childhood in the 1930s.* Chicago: Ivan R. Dee, 2005.

Lindsey, Treva B. *Colored No More: Reinventing Black Womanhood in Washington, D.C.* Champaign: University of Illinois Press, 2017.

———. "Configuring Modernities: New Negro Womanhood in the Nation's Capital, 1890–1940." PhD diss., Duke University, 2010.

Lipsitz, George. "The Racialization of Space and the Spatialization of Race: Theorizing the Hidden Architecture of Landscape." *Landscape Journal* 26 (January 2007): 10–23.

Longstreth, Richard. "The Unusual Transformation of Downtown Washington in the Early Twentieth Century." *Washington History* 13, no. 2 (Fall/Winter 2001–2): 50–71.

McKee, James B. *Sociology and the Race Problem: The Failure of a Perspective.* Champaign: University of Illinois Press, 1993.

McKittrick, Katherine. *Demonic Grounds: Black Women and the Cartographies of Struggle.* Minneapolis: University of Minnesota Press, 2006.

McKittrick, Katherine, and Clyde Woods, eds. *Black Geographies and the Politics of Place.* Cambridge, MA: South End Press, 2007.

McQuirter, Marya Annette. "Claiming the City: African Americans, Urbanization, and Leisure in Washington, D.C., 1902–1957." PhD diss., University of Michigan, 2000.

Meier, August. *A White Scholar and the Black Community, 1945–1965.* Amherst: University of Massachusetts Press, 1992.

Meier, August, and Elliott Rudwick. *Black History and the Historical Profession, 1915–1980.* Champaign: University of Illinois Press, 1986.

Mellis, Delia Cunningham. "The Monsters We Defy: Washington, D.C. in the Red Summer of 1919." PhD diss., City University of New York, Graduate Center, 2008.

Miller, Frederic M., and Howard Gillette Jr. "Race Relations in Washington, D.C., 1878–1955: A Photographic Essay." *Journal of Urban History* 21, no. 1 (1994): 57–85.

——. *Washington Seen: A Photographic History.* Baltimore: Johns Hopkins University Press, 1995.

Miller, James. "Black Washington and the New Negro." In *Composing Urban History and the Constitution of Civic Identities,* edited by John J. Czaplicka and Blair A. Ruble. Washington, DC: Woodrow Wilson Center; Baltimore: John Hopkins University Press, 2003.

Mintz, Steven. "A Historical Ethnography of Black Washington, D.C." *Columbia Historical Society* 52 (1989): 235–253.

——. *Huck's Raft: A History of American Childhood.* Cambridge, MA: Harvard University Press, 2004.

Mitchell, Don. *Cultural Geography: A Critical Introduction.* Oxford: Blackwell Publishers, 2000.

Mitchell, Michele. *Righteous Propagation: African Americans and the Politics of Racial Destiny after Reconstruction.* Chapel Hill: University of North Carolina Press, 2004.

Mitchell, Michele, Tera W. Hunter, and Sandra Gunning, eds. *Dialogues of Dispersal: Gender, Sexuality and African Diasporas.* Oxford: Blackwell Publishing, 2004.

Moore, Jacqueline M. *Leading the Race: The Transformation of the Black Elite in the Nation's Capital, 1880–1920.* Charlottesville: University of Virginia Press, 1999.

Moore, Shirley Ann Wilson. *To Place Our Deeds: The African American Community in Richmond, CA, 1910–1963.* Berkeley: University of California Press, 2000.

Morris, Aldon. "The Sociology of Race and W. E. B. DuBois and the Path Not Taken." In *Sociology in America: A History,* edited by Craig Calhoun. Chicago: University of Chicago Press, 2007.

Muhammad, Khalil Gibran. *The Condemnation of Blackness: Race, Crime, and the Making of Modern Urban America.* Cambridge, MA: Harvard University Press, 2011.

Nadell, Martha Jane. *Enter the New Negroes: Images of Race in American Culture.* Cambridge, MA: Harvard University Press, 2004.

Nasaw, David. *Children of the City: At Work and at Play.* New York: Oxford University Press, 1985.

Nieves, Angel David, and Leslie M. Alexander, eds. *"We Shall Independent Be": African American Place Making and the Struggle to Claim Space in the United States.* Boulder: University of Colorado Press, 2008.

O'Connor, Alice. *Poverty Knowledge: Social Science, Social Policy, and the Poor in Twentieth Century U.S. History.* Princeton, NJ: Princeton University, 2001.

Odem, Mary E. *Delinquent Daughters: Protecting and Policing Adolescent Female Sexuality in the United States, 1885–1920.* Chapel Hill: University of North Carolina Press, 1995.

Orbach, Barbara, and Nicholas Natanson. "The Mirror Image: Black Washington in World War II Era Federal Photography." *Washington History* 4, no. 1 (1992): 4–25.

Orleans, Peter, and William Russell Ellis Jr., eds. *Race, Change, and Urban Society.* Beverly Hills, CA: Sage Publications, 1971.

Pacifico, Michele F. "'Don't Buy Where You Can't Work': The New Negro Alliance of Washington." *Washington History* 6, no. 1 (Spring–Summer 1994): 66–88.

Painter, Nell Irvin. *Exodusters: Black Migration to Kansas after Reconstruction.* New York: Alfred A. Knopf, 1977.

Palmer, Phyllis. *Domesticity and Dirt: Housewives and Domestic Servants in the United States, 1920–1945.* Philadelphia: Temple University Press, 1989.

Paris, Jenell Williams. "'Fides' Means Faith: A Catholic Neighborhood House in Lower Northwest Washington, D.C." *Washington History* 11, no. 2 (Fall/Winter 1999–2000): 24–45.

Philips, Kimberley L. *Alabama North: African-American Migrants, Community, and Working Class Activism in Cleveland, 1915–45.* Urbana: University of Illinois Press, 1999.

Porter, Theodore, and Dorothy Ross, eds. *Cambridge History of Science*, vol. 7, *The Modern Social Sciences.* New York: Cambridge University Press, 2003.

Prince, Sabiyha. *African Americans and Gentrification in Washington, DC: Race, Class and Social Justice in the Nation's Capital.* Burlington, VT: Ashgate Publishing, 2014.

Quashie, Kevin. *The Sovereignty of Quiet: Beyond Resistance in Black Culture.* New Brunswick, NJ: Rutgers University Press, 2012.

Roberts, Samuel K., Jr. *Infectious Fear: Politics, Disease, and the Health Effects of Segregation.* Chapel Hill: University of North Carolina Press, 2009.

Robertson, Stephen. "See What I Mean? Media, Visual, and Spatial Evidence → Putting Harlem on the Map." In *Writing History in the Digital Age*, edited by Jack Dougherty and Kristen Nawrotzki. http://WritingHistory.trincoll.edu.

Robertson, Stephen, Shane White, Stephen Garton, and Graham White. "This Harlem Life: Black Families and Everyday Life in the 1920s and 1930s." *Journal of Social History* 1, no. 44 (Fall 2010): 97–122.

Roe, Donald. "The Dual School System in the District of Columbia, 1862–1954: Origins, Problems, Protests." *Washington History* 16, no. 2 (Fall/Winter 2004-5): 26–43.

Ross, Marlon. *Manning the Race: Reforming Black Men in the Jim Crow Era.* New York: New York University Press, 2004.

Sandage, Scott A. "A Marble House Divided: The Lincoln Memorial, the Civil Rights Movement, and the Politics of Memory, 1939–1963." *Journal of American History* 80, no. 1 (June 1993): 135–167.

Scott, Daryl Michael. *Contempt and Pity: Social Policy and the Image of the Damaged Black Psyche, 1880–1966.* Chapel Hill: University of North Carolina Press, 1997.

Scott, David. *Conscripts of Modernity: The Tragedy of Colonial Enlightenment.* Durham, NC: Duke University Press, 2004.

Scott, Joan. "The Evidence of Experience." *Critical Inquiry* 17, no. 4 (Summer 1991): 773—797.

Sewell, Jessica Ellen. *Women and the Everyday City: Public Space in San Francisco, 1890–1915.* Minneapolis: University of Minnesota Press, 2011.

Simmons, LaKisha Michelle. *Crescent City Girls: The Lives of Young Black Women in Segregated New Orleans.* Chapel Hill: University of North Carolina Press, 2015.

———. "'Justice Mocked': Violence and Accountability in New Orleans." *American Quarterly* 61, no. 3 (Sept. 2009): 477–498.

Sitkoff, Harvard. *A New Deal for Blacks: The Emergence of Civil Rights as a National Issue.* New York: Oxford University Press, 1978.

Smith, Andrea. "Heteroglossia, 'Commonsense,' and Social Memory." *American Ethnologist* 31, no. 2 (May 2004): 251–269.

Smith, Kathryn Schneider, ed. *Washington at Home: An Illustrated History of Neighborhoods in the Nation's Capital.* Baltimore: Johns Hopkins University Press, 2010.

Smith, Neil. "Contours of a Spatialized Politics: Homeless Vehicles and the Production of Geographical Scale." *Social Text* 33 (1992): 54–81.

Smith, Neil, and Setha Low, eds. *The Politics of Public Space.* New York: Routledge, 2006.

Stewart, Alison. *First Class: The Legacy of Dunbar, America's First Black Public High School.* Chicago: Lawrence Hill Books, 2013.

Stuckey, Sterling. *Slave Culture: Nationalist Theory and the Foundations of Black America.* New York: Oxford University Press, 1987.

Sullivan, Patricia. *Days of Hope: Race and Democracy in the New Deal Era.* Chapel Hill: University of North Carolina Press, 1996.

Summers, Martin. *Manliness and Its Discontents: The Black Middle Class and the Transformation of Masculinity, 1900–1930.* Chapel Hill: University of North Carolina Press, 2004.

Thomas, Deborah. *Exceptional Violence: Embodied Citizenship in Transnational Jamaica.* Durham, NC: Duke University Press, 2011.

Thurber, Ben Henry. "The Negro at the Nation's Capital, 1913–1921." PhD diss., Yale University, 1973.

Thursz, Daniel. *Where Are They Now? A Study of the Impact of Relocation on Former Residents of Southwest Washington Who Were Served in an HWC Demonstration Project.* Washington, DC: Health and Welfare Council of the National Capital Area, November 1966.

Trotter, Joe W., Jr., ed. *Black Milwaukee: The Making of an Industrial Proletariat, 1915–1945.* Champaign: University of Illinois Press, 1985.

———. *The Great Migration in Historical Perspective: New Dimensions of Race, Class, and Gender.* Bloomington: Indiana University Press, 1991.

White, Ed. *The Backcountry and the City: Colonization and Conflict in Early America.* Minneapolis: University of Minnesota Press, 2005.

Wilkerson, Isabel. *The Warmth of Other Suns: The Epic Story of America's Great Migration.* New York: Random House, 2010.

Williams, Kim Protho. *The D.C. Historic Alley Buildings Survey.* Washington, DC: DC Historic Preservation Office, 2014.

Williams, Paul K. *Images of America: Southwest Washington, D.C.* Charleston, SC: Arcadian Publishing, 2005.

Williams, Raymond. *Marxism and Literature.* New York: Oxford University Press, 1977.

Williams, Vernon J., Jr. *From Caste to a Minority: Changing Attitudes of American Sociologists toward Afro-Americans, 1896–1945*. Westport, CT: Greenwood Press, 1989.

———. *Rethinking Race: Franz Boas and His Contemporaries*. Lexington: University of Kentucky Press, 1996.

Wilson, David. *Inventing Black-on-Black Violence: Discourse, Space, and Representation*. New York: Syracuse University Press, 2005.

Wilson, Francille Rusan. "'This Past Was Waiting for Me When I Came': The Contextualization of Black Women's History." *Feminist Studies* 22, no. 2 (Summer 1996): 346–361.

———. *The Segregated Scholars: Black Social Scientists and the Creation of Black Labor Studies, 1890–1950*. Charlottesville: University of Virginia Press, 2006.

Wilson, Sondra Kathryn, ed. *The Opportunity Reader: Stories, Poetry, and Essays from the Urban League's Opportunity Magazine*. New York: Modern Library, 1999.

Winkler, Erin N. *Learning Race, Learning Place: Shaping Racial Identities and Ideas in African American Childhoods*. New Brunswick, NJ: Rutgers University Press, 2012.

Wolcott, David B. *Cops and Kids: Policing Juvenile Delinquency in Urban America, 1890–1940*. Columbus: Ohio State University Press, 2005.

Wolcott, Virginia. *Remaking Respectability: African American Women in Interwar Detroit*. Chapel Hill: University of North Carolina Press, 2001.

Yellin, Eric S. "'It Was Still No South to Us': African American Civil Servants at the Fin de Siècle." *Washington History* 21 (2009): 22–47.

INDEX

ABOUT THE AUTHOR

Paula C. Austin is Assistant Professor of History and African American Studies at Boston University. She writes and teaches about black visual culture and African American and civil rights history, and facilitates faculty professional development on diversity, equity, and inclusion.